Green Friendship Bridge

Advances Freedom and Peace
with Mexico and Central America

Mark R. Edwards

Green Friendship Bridge
Advances Freedom and Peace
with Mexico and Central America

Mark R. Edwards

Vision: Advance freedom, peace and friendship while enhancing homeland security by enabling families in Mexico and Central America to produce healthy and nutritious food locally with a green friendship bridge made of peace microfarms.

The Green Friendship Bridge distributes 14,000 peace microfarms throughout Mexico and Central America

Give Ana food and satisfy her hunger for a day.

Teach Ana to grow abundant food in Peace Microfarms,

And Ana can feed her family and her community for generations.

Enable Ana to share her knowledge, and Ana can feed the world.

Comments to: *drmetrics@gmail.com*

The Green Friendship Bridge Advances Freedom and Peace

Dedication

*To the millions malnourished children in Mexico, Central America
and Rural USA. May they find restored health and food security.*

 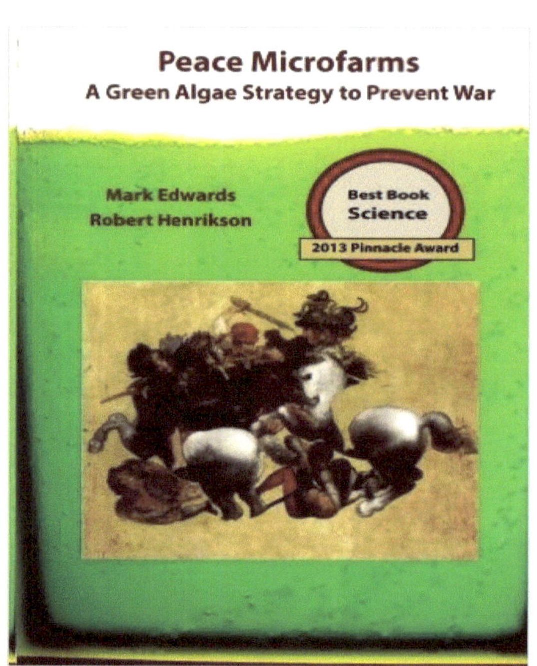

Algae Microfarms and Peace Microfarms provide a path for ending malnutrition

Robert Henrikson's *Algae Microfarms: for home, school, community and urban gardens, rooftop, mobile and vertical farms and living buildings* shows the value of algae microfarms for families, farmers and community.

Peace Microfarms: A green Algae Strategy to Prevent War (Edwards), explains how algae microfarms give growers the freedom to produce food, feed and other valuable bioproducts locally. Microfarms prevent war by using abundance production methods that save scarce natural resources for or next generation.

ISBN-13: 978-1981300969

ISBN-10: 1981300961

Cover: Monet's Bridge with waterlilies.

Green Friendship Bridge may be used under Creative Common License for education.

Green Friendship Bridge

The Green Friendship Bridge proposes to shift 1% of the cost for Trump's proposed wall with Mexico to build 14,000 peace microfarms. The Bridge will advance freedom and peace in place of an ugly barrier. The microfarms, provided with training to farmers and families scattered across Mexico and Central America, will create jobs, reduce malnutrition and improve health. Peace microfarms will enable families to produce good food locally so they do not have to migrate north. U.S. farm policies, especially commodity subsidies and NAFTA, forced much of the migration. Peace microfarms will reduce forced migration and provide substantial benefits for all.

Social

- Beautiful microfarms versus an ugly wall.
- Educate new generations in sustainability.
- Grow delicious, nutritious food locally.
- Build social equity; employ handicapped.

Economic

- Farmers profit and can stay on their land.
- Allow communities to sustain themselves.
- Employ women, handicapped and elderly.
- Improve field crop yields and quality >20%.

Environmental

- Enable sustainable local food production.
- Save 25% of cropland, fresh water and fuel.
- Cut inorganic fertilizer pollution by >60%.
- Cut GHG, black smoke pollution >80%.

Healthy foods

- Better taste and sensory appeal.
- High nutralence, nutrient density
- Naturally diverse with no GMO materials.
- Clean, no pesticide or other poison residue.

Health

- Eliminate malnutrition for 19 million children.
- Support healthy pregnant mothers.
- Fight the epidemic of obesity and diabetes.
- Detox heavy metal poisoning for millions.

Ecology

- Reclaim 500,000 hectares of cropland.
- Restore porosity to compacted soil.
- Dissolve embedded salts and infertility.
- Reduce agricultural pollution by >60%.

Disaster relief

- Provide sustainable healthy food in a few weeks.
- Improve health and vitality for communities.
- Recycle nutrients to produce clean water.
- Produce valuable nutraceuticals and medicines.

U.S. Green Friendship Bridge

- Eliminate malnutrition for 6 million U.S. children.
- Support healthy pregnant mothers.
- Improve health for military service.
- Fight the epidemic of obesity and diabetes.

The *Green Friendship Bridge* reinforces American values rather than wasting more money on an ineffective and unsightly border wall.

The value proposition for eliminating malnutrition for over 19 million children and pregnant mothers dwarfs the value of additional wall. The total value set for Mexico and Central America is so substantial that we will need to build a sister Green Bridge for U.S. families in impoverished rural areas and urban food deserts. Over 20% of U.S. children are food insecure and obesity and diabetes create a $150 billion annual drag on America. The U.S. Green Friendship Bridge can resolve food security, malnutrition, obesity and diabetes for millions of Americans.

Table of Contents

1. Can Peace Microfarms Trump Trump's Fence with Mexico?

A border wall along 1,954 miles, (3,145 km) of the U.S. — Mexico border undermines national security, wastes money and promotes an incredibly ugly American image.

The U.S. can improve national security significantly and create a very positive image by a simple policy change. Use 1% of the wall cost to build a Green Friendship Bridge composed of 14,000 peace microfarms for Mexican and Central American farmers. This bridge offers substantial advantages compared with erecting a border wall that experts and politicians agree would not stop illegal traffic.

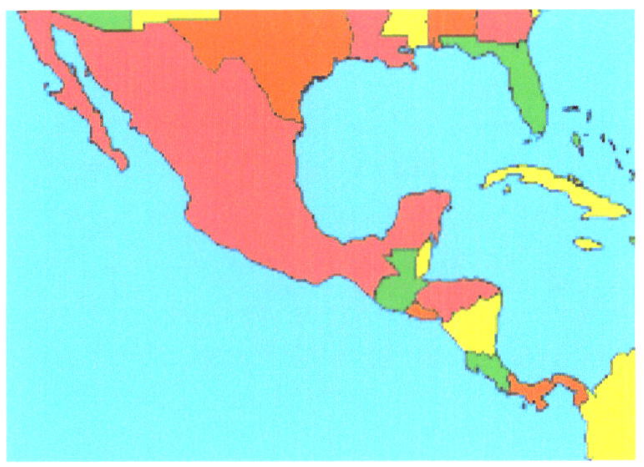

Peace microfarms will be sprinkled throughout Mexico and Central America

Trump's proposed wall

Donald Trump: *"I would build a great wall, and nobody builds walls better than me, believe me, and I'll build them very inexpensively — I will build a great, great wall on our southern border. And I will have Mexico pay for that wall. Mark my words."*

Donald Trump repeated his claim during the 25 February 2016 presidential debate that he would build a fence and make Mexico pay for the wall to curb illegal immigration. Mr. Trump's border wall has become a contentious symbol of his campaign. His pledge to make Mexico pay for it has drawn

fierce denunciations from Mexican leaders who have vowed never to pony up a dime.

Mexico's ex-president Vicente Fox reacted to Trump's proposal to build a wall separating the two countries. "I told him: I am not going to pay for this f**** wall," Fox said during an interview with journalist Jorge Ramos for Univisión. When a slew of objections came from Mexican leaders, Trump said, "The wall just got 10 feet higher."

Donald Trump issued a memo saying he would force Mexico to pay for a border wall by threatening to cut off billions of dollars in remittances sent by immigrants living in the U.S. Trump threatened to change a rule under the USA Patriot Act, an anti-terrorism law, to cut off funds sent to Mexico through money transfers known as remittances. Trump said he would withdraw the threat if Mexico makes "a one-time payment of $5-10 billion" to finance the wall."

Building a wall to keep out illegal immigrants is not a novel plan. About 670 miles of fencing on the U.S.-Mexico border was completed in accordance with the Bush administration's Secure Fence Act of 2006. The first section of steel fencing built on relatively easy terrain cost about $2.4 billion.

Cost

The Senate Homeland Security Committee said in an April 2017 report that costs could soar to **$70 billion** — not including the significant costs and legal resources required for land acquisition. Official estimates also fail to include road-building and earth and drainage work, labor costs, land acquisition costs, surveillance equipment and border patrol personnel. Wall maintenance would likely cost another several billion a year.

Marc Rosenblum, deputy director of the U.S. Immigration Policy Program at the Migration Policy Institute estimates construction of the rest of the border wall would take a minimum of 10 years. He anticipates the final cost will be substantially higher than the GAO estimate.

The cost for Trump's wall will be substantially higher because the existing border barrier is a fence, not a wall. If Trump really wants to build a wall, the price would at least double. In addition, the 670 miles of current fencing would have to be replaced. In some areas, the current barrier is not even fencing, but only vehicular barriers.

A wall would require massive amounts of cement and rebar. The cement would probably come from Mexico and the rebar from China, due to insufficient production in the U.S. Experts have pointed out that there is not enough water in the arid border sections to make enough cement for a wall. The water limitation alone makes the wall problematic.

Former Homeland Security Secretary Michael Chertoff waived 36 federal laws to build the existing wall. In addition to environmental laws, he swept aside the Farmland Protection Policy Act, the Religious Freedom Restoration Act, and the Native American Graves Protection and Repatriation Act. The environmental laws are in place to protect endangered animals and local ecosystems. Secretary Chertoff waived all those laws because he knew that border walls would violate them.

Joe Romm, editor of Climate Progress, observed that the border runs straight down the middle of 1,254 snaking miles of the Rio Grande River, causing extreme siting problems.

Trump's Interior Secretary, Ryan Zinke suggested the wall would be built on Mexico's side of the river. If the wall were on the US side; the US would cede the Rio Grande River to Mexico, which is not going to happen. Mexico has said forcefully that the wall will not be built on Mexican land.

Similarly, the Tohono O'odham Nation's reservation spans 75 miles of the US-Mexico border. Tribal leaders have stated unequivocally that the Tohono O'odham Nation does not support the wall. Tribal leaders criticized the Trump White House for signing an executive order without consulting the tribe. Tribal member Bradley Moreno said "It's going to affect our sacred lands. It's going to affect our ceremonial sites. It's going to affect the environment. We have wildlife, and they have their own patterns of migration. There are just so many things that are wrong with this. The whole idea behind it is just racist." A tribal vice-chairman declared the government would build the wall "over my dead body."

Extreme weather and climate change make both the siting and design challenges unimaginably greater and substantially more expensive. The devastating Texas storms in May 2015 dropped 35 trillion gallons of water and deluged the state. The National Weather Service in Fort Worth estimated that was enough to cover the entire state 8 inches deep. Flooding rivers and flash floods through desert arroyos would have destroyed large sections of a wall.

A 2015 study concluded that anthropogenic global warming contributed to the physical processes that caused the persistent precipitation in May 2015." NOAA reported that in some areas, the deluge was "greater than a 1-in-1000-year event." No less than of 18 major flood events have hit Texas, Louisiana, Oklahoma, Arkansas since March 2015. Extreme weather events have become common and current wall designs will not hold up to severe storms. The 2017 hurricane season featured 17 named storms with Harvey, Irma, and Maria, that did a total of over $360 billion in damage.

DHS officers have pointed out repeatedly that border fences in remote locations do nothing, other than annoy border crossers. The fence does not stop people from going over or under the barrier.

Both Democrats and Republicans have testified that the U.S. has all the fencing needed.

Borders

People cross the U.S. border illegally with the hope of getting better jobs to provide food for their families. Subsidized U.S. crops, especially corn, have destroyed the ability of many foreign farmers to make a living. Most of Haiti's farmers went bankrupt decades ago from U.S. food aid that dumped grains on Haiti's economy at prices lower than farmers could produce. Now Haiti is dependent on subsidized U.S. grain.

NAFTA Trade Agreement

Similarly, over 1.5 million Mexican farmers were forced to leave their land because they could not compete with subsidized U.S. corn. NAFTA sealed a trade agreement but left untouched the serious problem of U.S. crop subsidies that undermine Mexican (and Canadian) farmers. Many of these farmers added their feet to the flow of illegal immigrants to the U.S. from Mexico. Homeland Security should consider joining the World Trade Organization where several countries, including Mexico and Canada, are suing to end U.S. crop subsidies.

America's values

The border wall is an embarrassment to every American who cheered with the breaking of the Berlin Wall. In a speech at the Brandenburg Gate commemorating the 750th anniversary of

Berlin in June 1987, President Ronald Reagan challenged Mikhail Gorbachev, then the General Secretary of the Communist Party of the Soviet Union, to tear down the wall as a symbol of increasing freedom in the Eastern Bloc.

A border wall conflicts with core American values. Our symbol of liberty, the Statue of Liberty, contains Emma Lazarus' Famous Poem, which says:

> Give me your tired, your poor,
> Your huddled masses yearning to breathe free,
> The wretched refuse of your teeming shore.
> Send these, the homeless, tempest-tossed to me,
> I lift my lamp beside the golden door!

President Regan said: "We welcome change and openness; for we believe that freedom and security go together, that the advance of human liberty can only strengthen the cause of world peace.

There is one sign the Soviets can make that would be unmistakable, that would advance dramatically the cause of freedom and peace.

General Secretary Gorbachev, if you seek peace, if you seek prosperity for the Soviet Union and Eastern Europe, if you seek liberalization, come here to this gate. *Mr. Gorbachev, open this gate. Mr. Gorbachev, tear down this wall!*"

The Berlin Wall

Yet 30 years later, the U.S. fails to advance human liberty and instead erects a hideous wall to keep foreigners out. Donald Trump wants to spend billions more to build out the wall.

Friendship Bridge

Rather than waste money on 1300 miles of ugly wall, why not build a Green Friendship Bridge? The Friendship Bridge proposed here would shift the cost of only 1% of the wall, (13 miles) for a total of $700 million, to finance the Green Friendship Bridge. The bridge would be composed of microfarms scattered across Mexico and Central America. Peace microfarms will create jobs, reduce or eradicate malnutrition, improve health as well as enable farmers and families to produce good food locally so they do not have to migrate north. The Green Friendship Bridge project can be initiated for a small fraction of $700 million. The larger cost will allow gifting Peace Microfarms rather than using microloans and other mechanisms to finance microfarm diffusion.

Friendship Bridges have been built in many ways. Microloans and education create Friendship Bridges that empower Guatemalan women to create their own solutions to poverty for themselves, their families and their communities. The Gates Foundation has built Friendship Bridges in many countries with projects to empower people locally to improve the health and prosperity for people and their communities.

Child malnutrition

Child hood malnutrition is a global issue. The November 2017 *Global Nutrition Report* found that hunger statistics are going in the wrong direction. Tonight, 815 million people will to bed hungry, up from 777 million in 2015. The global community is grappling with multiple burdens of malnutrition as 88% of countries face the serious burden of two or three forms of malnutrition, childhood stunting, anemia in women of reproductive age and/or overweight in adult women. In poor areas of Mexico and Central America, more than 50% of the mothers and children are malnourished.

Antenna Technologies provides an excellent model for distributing the knowledge and technology for building Friendship Bridges. Antenna Technologies is a Swiss foundation committed to the scientific research of technological, health and economic solutions in partnership with universities, non-profit organizations and private companies to meet the basic needs of marginalized populations in developing countries. Antenna is active in the local production and distribution of spirulina, a microalga of high nutritional value. A daily dose of just a few grams can lead to spectacular improvements in the nutritional state of malnourished children. Antenna pursues awareness and information activities on nutrition and spirulina.

Child malnutrition is the single biggest contributor to under-five mortality due to greater susceptibility to infections and slow recovery from illness. The World Bank reports that in several countries in Central America, over 50% of children under 5 are malnourished. One major outcome of malnutrition is stunting – low height for a child's age, which affects almost half of children in Latin America. One in five stunting cases is due to poor growth during fetal life. Malnutrition during fetal life results in failure of the major organs to develop properly, which is not treatable after birth.

Child malnutrition causes significant cognitive impairments and serious health problems throughout life. Studies show that stunted children in the first two years of life have lower cognitive test scores, delayed enrolment, higher absenteeism and more class repetition compared with non-stunted children. Vitamin A deficiency reduces immunity and increases the incidence and gravity of infectious diseases resulting in increased school absenteeism. Child malnutrition impacts on economic productivity. The mental impairment caused by iodine deficiency is permanent and directly linked to productivity loss. The loss from stunting is calculated as 1.38% reduced productivity for every 1% decrease in height.

Maternal malnutrition increases the risk of poor pregnancy outcomes including obstructed labor, premature or low-birth-weight babies and postpartum hemorrhage. Severe anemia during pregnancy is linked to increased mortality at labor. Low-birth-weight is a significant contributor to infant mortality. Growth-retarded adult women are likely to carry on the vicious cycle of malnutrition by giving birth to low birth-weight babies.

Algae solution

Antenna Technologies research shows that on an annual basis, a 1 m^2 tank yields a production of 6 g/ day, which sums to 2 kg of dried spirulina a year.

- Each m^2 cultivated can supply a cure for 20 children with nutritional deficiencies.

- Each m^2 cultivated can supply sufficient critical nutrients for 20 pregnant women or mothers nursing newborns.

- The cure for a malnourished child lasts for 6 to 8 weeks, using 2 g of spirulina a day, thus requiring only => 100 g of spirulina. The spirulina may be dried, fresh or frozen.

Spirulina provides substantial health benefits for people of all ages. The phycocyanin, polysaccharides, antioxidants and phytonutrients in a 3-gram spirulina serving per day:

- Restores and enhances beneficial intestinal flora.

- Promotes and stimulates immune system protection.

- Strengthens neuro-protection and promotes anti-aging.

- Enhances body's own healing response with phycobilins.

- Detoxifies pollutants, heavy metals, radioactive compounds.

- Improves eye and cell health with antioxidants and carotenoids.

Growers can produce fresh, frozen or dried spirulina. Microfarmers in the U.S. typically sell 100 grams, (3.5 oz) of spirulina for about $20. Fresh or frozen spirulina may bring 2x higher prices. French, Spanish, U.S. and Asian microfarmers are supplementing their income by selling spirulina in their community.

A standard algae microfarm may cost $40,000 in materials and use local labor. Microfarm accessories may add another $10,000. Therefore, 13 miles of Trump's wall cost can finance 14,000 peace microfarms. Further detail on how the microfarms are built will follow.

We expect to lower the cost by more than 50% and triple productivity within three years. Most the productivity improvements will come from the growers who share their insights through the Green Mastermind Network that includes microfarmers, students, scientists, academics and commercial algae experts. We plan to build modular microfarms in a container that can be shipped immediately anywhere in the world. A microfarm in a box can be assembled in a day and be producing right away.

Operation of a modest microfarm requires about 2 hours, three times a week. Operation requires only modest physical labor and no heavy equipment. Microfarmers have no exposure to dust, pesticides or agricultural poisons. While industrial agriculture creates high physical risk for farmers, microfarms have near-zero physical risk. Industrial farmers incur substantial risk of crop failure from weather, drought and pests. A severe storm my interrupt microfarm production during the storm, but production can begin again almost immediately.

Terrestrial farmers typically produce only one food crop a year, which ripens towards the end of the growing season in the Fall. Their family may be very hungry the rest of the year. When their crop fails or yield drops, the farmer and family face severe economic stress and hunger. A microfarmer produce year-round in mild climates. Pests may destroy a culture, but the microfarm can be cleaned and the begin producing more food in a few weeks. New technologies are reducing the impact of pests for microfarmers.

Microfarms are designed for simple operation, which minimizes the learning curve. Microfarms can be operated by women, elderly and handicapped people. This broad access to food production allows for social justice, where people have equitable access to food production and healthy food.

Note to DIY microfarmers. Single microfarms typically require a larger investment. This project plans to source materials in bulk. Robert Henrikson created an excellent "Getting started checklist" for people interesting in building a microfarm.

Value?

What is the value proposition for the Green Friendship Bridge versus Trump's wall?

	Friendship Bridge	Trump's Wall
Visual meaning	Friendship	Hostility
Message	Peace and goodwill	Hostility
Action	Liberty	Control
Construction	Polycarbonate	Concrete
Image	Beautiful	Ugly
Usefulness	Excellent	Poor
Sustainable	Yes	25 years
Social and economic	Strong	None
Farmers / families	Strong	None
Economic benefits for communities	High	Negative
Hunger and poverty	Strong	None
Resolves childhood malnutrition	Strong	None
Benefits mothers	Strong	None
Improves health	Strong	None
Local ecology	Strong	None
Reduces waste and pollution	Strong	None
Cost	$700 million	$70 B plus
Maintenance/year	$1 million	$3 billion
Construction time	3 years	10 years
Homeland Security	Strong	Poor
For America	Strong	Awful

Summary

A Friendship Bridge constructed with thousands of peace microfarms sited throughout Mexico and Central America would give farmers an opportunity to support their family and community. Since peace microfarms require only modest physical labor, women, the physically handicapped and elderly people could grow highly nutritious food locally. Peace microfarms enable social justice, where all people have equitable access to the resources for growing food. Families could support themselves and stay in the communities they love.

The highly nutritious algae offer a wide variety of delicious and healthy foods. One peace microfarm can support a community's need for vital nutrition for babies and young children as well as for their mothers. Strong nutrition can avoid low birthweight babies, stunting and cognitive loss for children. Many older people that suffer from malnutrition can recover their normal lives with algae-based nutrients that are easily bioabsorbed by the body. Prior Algae Secrets posts described the ability of spirulina and other algae species to chelate with heavy metals such as lead, mercury and arsenic and cleanse the brain and body of these poisons. A single community microfarm would provide sufficient algae to safely remove these poisons.

Healthier families improve economic outcomes. Peace microfarms can provide jobs for farmers and their families so they can continue to live and thrive in their home communities.

2. Can Peace Microfarms Build a Green Friendship Bridge?

Peace microfarms will enable farmers and families to grow food, feed, biofertilizers and healthy nutritional products on tiny land footprints so they can stay home and not be forced by economics to migrate north. Funding equals just 13 miles of additional border wall.

The 2017 DHS $40.6 billion budget does not include funding for The Green Friendship Bridge project. However, the Friendship Bridge offers substantial advantages compared with erecting even 13 miles of additional border wall. Numerous experts, including Congressional members from both parties, have stated the obvious: a longer wall will neither improve Homeland Security nor slow illegal immigration.

Resource concentration

The Friendship Bridge addresses a global challenge, equitable access to diminishing natural resources. Income inequality, profits, assets and control have flowed to the top 0.1% since the 1980s. This flow has substantially increased centralization of resource control, creating scarcity for many where there could be abundance for all.

The world needs decentralized production and distribution solutions for sustainable and affordable food. Peace microfarms decentralize food production and enable farmers and families to grow excellent food locally.

Peace microfarms

Many experts have written articles and books about how past, current and future wars will be fought over diminishing natural resources, e.g. fertile soil, fresh water, fossil fuels, fertilizer and agricultural chemicals. People are willing to take extremely drastic action to acquire sufficient food for their family.

Peace microfarms provide an alternative to war over natural resources. Microfarms grow healthy and affordable food using no or minimal fossil resources. Compared with hording natural resources or huge military spending, peace microfarms offer a substantially less expensive solution to avoid war.

Over 30 books about coming resource wars

Peace microfarms enable growers to practice **abundance,** with the goal to recover, recycle and reuse carbon and other nutrients multiple times. Abundance improves crop quality and productivity substantially while systematically cleaning ecosystems. Abundance growers view waste streams as nutrient gold mines that are too valuable to discard into ecosystems. Cycling nutrients substantially reduces the cost of food production.

Modern industrial agriculture uses "one-and-done" consumption. Farmers must buy a new set of crop inputs every year, with little or no nutrient cycling. Abundance agriculture will revitalize opportunities for farmers and help them restore fertility to their fields. Sustainable food and energy production will improve life quality for farm families, communities and their nation.

The Victory Gardens that were popular during World War II encouraged families to produce food locally, often in their backyard. Unfortunately, 72-years later, many people in Mexico and Central America cannot grow Victory Gardens because the inputs are too expensive or not available. Most families have insufficient fertile soil, fresh water, fossil fuels, inorganic fertilizer or pesticides to grow food for their family or community.

Abundance growers produce freedom foods, nutritious and delicious food with minimal fossil, (non-renewable) resources. Peace microfarms have the unique ability to recover and repurpose waste stream nutrients into healthy food, biofeed, biofertilizer and other valuable bioproducts. Microfarms do not need cropland because the culture grows in a raceway, (container) that can be sited nearly anywhere. Growers may use non-potable water, such as waste, brine or even seawater. Microfarms need minimal energy for mixing the culture and harvest, which can be supplied by green sources. Algae can recover most the nutrients needed from waste streams, so that avoids the high cost of buying fertilizer. Microfarmers can cultivate excellent crops consistently without the need for agricultural pesticides and poisons.

Peace microfarms do not require heavy machinery or heavy labor, which makes food production safe for young, elderly and even handicapped people. Algae microfarms can produce a wide variety of algae cultivars. Microfarms tend to focus on high protein and often produce the easily grown spirulina, which grows naturally today, in nearly every country in the world.

Spirulina

The FAO reported recently that spirulina shows a significant potential for fighting chronic malnutrition and for economic development. A FAO 2008 report said "International organizations working with spirulina should consider preparing a practical guide to small-scale spirulina production. This small-scale production should be orientated towards:

- Providing nutritional supplements for widespread use in rural and urban communities where the staple diet is poor or inadequate;

- Allowing diversification from traditional crops in cases where land or water resources are limited."

"There is a role for both national governments – as well as intergovernmental organizations – to reevaluate the potential of spirulina to fulfill both their own food security needs as well as a tool for their overseas development […]" China has recognized spirulina as a national food.

Many climates in Mexico and Central America can grow spirulina year-round. Spirulina can be grown and consumed locally. There is no need to conserve it, although it is easily dried in the sun. Fresh spirulina can be eaten directly without any processing or cooking, eliminating costly energy consumption.

Mexico and Central American famers share numerous factors that make peace microfarms a logical choice. Huge U.S. subsidies have made corn and some other food staples so cheap that famers cannot produce food grains profitably. Rural areas especially suffer from high unemployment and youth unemployment in Central America exceeds 24%. Each country in Central America has areas where over 50% of children under five are severely malnourished. The numbers for the elderly are even worse. Each country experiences severe climate chaos, water shortages and expanding deserts, that limit crop production. Central America has the highest levels of soil degradation in the world, reported at roughly 75%. Fertility depletion and erosion from water and wind have left many families with tiny plots of nearly non-arable land. Peace microfarms may be the only solution that addresses each of these issues.

Microfarm advantages

Whether farmers choose to grow spirulina, chlorella or a local indigenous algae species, microfarms offer a valuable set of social, health, economic and environmental benefits.

Social benefits

Microfarms provide substantial social benefits, including the following.

Beautiful image. The visual image of green growing systems supporting families and community trumps an ugly border wall.

Education. Green solar gardens provide an excellent opportunity for training people throughout the region in sustainable farming practices. Peace microfarms are learning environments where lateral learning thrives as microfarmers share their insights and experience.

Produce food locally. Many areas are not suitable for farming. Microfarms can grow healthy and delicious food nearly anywhere there is sunshine. Advanced growers can supplement solar energy with high-efficiency LED lighting using controlled environment agriculture.

Employ women, youth, handicapped and elderly. Peace microfarms do not require heavy labor, which enable women, youth, handicapped and elderly to grow heathy food.

Health benefits

Eliminate childhood malnutrition. Many families are food insecure and do not get sufficient nutrients. In El Salvador, Guatemala, Honduras, and Nicaragua, over 50% of children under five are malnourished. A single microfarm can provide the critical nutrients for an entire community.

Support pregnant mothers. Pregnant mothers who get insufficient nutrients from their diet often deliver low birthweight babies, many of whom become stunted and intellectually challenged. Microfarms can provide sufficient nutrients to support healthy mothers and babies.

Eliminate pesticide pollution. Only about 1% of agricultural poisons are absorbed by the pest targets. Some of the remainder escapes the field and pollutes local communities. Substantial residuals may remain on produce even after washing. Peace microfarms can clean the local environment rather than polluting.

Detox heavy metal poisoning. Global warming amplifies water shortages that are addressed with deeper wells. Research shows that deeper wells tend to increase levels of heavy metal poisons including especially lead, mercury and arsenic. Eating algae foods allows the body to bioabsorb the tiny algae cells that chelate with heavy metals which are then passed out of the body in the urine.

Economic benefits

The economic benefits begin by allowing farmers and families to stay on their land.

Farmers and family profit. Peace microfarms enable farmers and families to make enough money to stay on their land.

Disaster relief. Climate chaos amplifies wildfires and fierce storms that create ecological and economic disasters. A common element of disaster is an abundance of wastewater but no clean water and no

fresh food. Peace microfarms can be delivered to disasters sites quickly and provide clean water and fresh food locally in a matter of weeks.

Recover worn out cropland. Algae biofertilizer has demonstrated the ability to restore degraded and even unfertile land and regenerate fertility. Algae biofertilizer applied through irrigation or spaying continues to grow green biomass in fields as long as moisture is available. The algae become humus like the application of organic mulch. **Note:** Algae biofertilizers and soil restoration may require growing multiple algae species.

Restore compacted soil. Large areas of desert cropland have become seriously compacted due to cultivation and punishment from heavy agricultural equipment. Crops cannot grow because the soil is to tight to allow roots to grow. Algae biofertilizers have demonstrated the ability to improve soil porosity, looseness, by 500%.

Dissolve embedded salts. Substantial areas of cropland are infertile due to salt invasion and the land must be abandoned because the salt kills rooted crops. Algae have no roots and algae biofertilizers have been shown to improve soil porosity so that salts can percolate with rain or irrigation below the root line.

Environmental benefits

Microfarms create sustainable food and energy while improving local ecosystems.

Sustainable local food production. Microfarms offer a very efficient and productive method for sustainable food production that consumes few non-renewable resources and delivers a positive carbon and environmental footprint.

Save cropland. Peace microfarms grow in containers that may be sited on non-arable land or where soil fertility has been degraded. Growers can also use rooftops, parking lots, hillsides, train right of ways, deserts or other locations not suitable for field crops.

Save water. Microfarms consume only modest amounts of water compared with field crops. Some models can reclaim wastewater.

Eliminate fertilizer pollution. Only about half of agricultural fertilizers are absorbed by crops. The rest blows or flow to waste streams causing serious pollution of waterways. The only thing microfarms emit to the environment is pure oxygen.

Save fuel. Peace microfarms may operate with no or minimal fossil fuels. Some operate off-the-grid using green power sources.

Reduce black smoke pollution. Microfarms do not use the heavy diesel equipment that emits huge amounts of black particulates. Local food production reduces carbon and particulate pollution emitted by trucks and trains.

Peace microfarms offer a new form of food production called Freedom Foods, which are free of fossil resources including fertile soil, fresh water, fossil fuels, fertilizers and pesticides. Freedom food production mimics nature by growing excellent food, and at the same time improving the environment to benefit future generations.

How?

How will the Friendship Bridge product proceed? The project will rely on the Algae Ambassadors selected from the *Algae Industry Magazine 2015 and 2017 International Polls* for design and direction. This team, supplemented by additional volunteers, has decades of experience in designing, building and operating peace microfarms.

The 14,000 microfarm sites may be selected by lottery after the design team determines how many microfarms are allocated to each country. Site selection will take into consideration local geography and climate. Most locations with adequate solar exposure will be eligible, independent of altitude. Spacing is important because each microfarm will want singular access to the local community for algae-based foods and bioproducts. Peace microfarms spaced at minimum of 20 miles apart, except in large cities, should allow each microfarm to flourish.

The process will need to create careful policy elements to assure the opportunity aligns with the culture of each region. Microfarmers will need to have skin in the game, possibly by paying a small percentage of their produce revenue to the Friendship Bridge Cooperative. Microfarmers will also be expected to attend trainings and pass a competency test. Tom Dempster, manager of

ATP3 based at Arizona State University, conducts a similar model microfarm training at Santa Fe Community College. Aaron Wolf Baum also conducts excellent algae starter workshops.

Robert Henrikson and his Smart Microfarms designs

Educational materials

An excellent set of educational materials for microfarmers has already been created. Robert Henrikson, an Algae Ambassador, has conducted research on spirulina since he served as CEO of Earthrise Nutraceuticals in the late 1970s. His work provides a clear path forward for the Friendship Bridge. Robert has been building Smart Microfarms along the West Coast for several years, producing spirulina and conducting research on the most productive operational methods and technologies. These systems are smart because they have remote monitors and controllers that can be networked across multiple growing systems.

Robert wrote an excellent 5-part series on algae microfarms for *Algae Industry Magazine*. Robert manages several free websites dedicated to promoting algae microfarms, spirulina and the future of our global society:

SmartMicrofarms.com – focuses on how to build and operate microfarms locally and how to network systems for cooperative assistance.

SpirulinaSource.com – provides exceptional resources including scientific research on the social, economic and nutrition value of spirulina.

AlgaeCompetition.com – provide visuals and examples of our algae future for food, feeds, medicines and living buildings. The Algae Competition was a global challenge to design visionary algae food and energy systems. The site includes fabulous graphics of algae microfarms as well as attractive algae recipes.

Microfarm field research has benefited from the assistance of engineers and scientists, notably Jean-Paul Jourdan, in developing a method of growing spirulina at the local level, simply and effectively. Simple methods of cultivating spirulina are especially suited to developing countries and to the environments with hot and desert climates. Recent books provide considerable guidance for microfarmers.

Growers can produce a wide range valuable bioproducts using no or minimal fossil resources. Communities and countries do not have the go to war over precious farm land, water, fuel, fertilizers or other agricultural inputs. Francisco Monteverde, a senior executive at Grupo Carso, graciously translated *Peace Microfarms* into Spanish, which will benefit microfarmers is Spanish-speaking countries.

Summary

A Green Friendship Bridge provides a beautiful alternative to a $70 billion border wall. The 14,000 peace microfarms sprinkled throughout Mexico and Central America will become a superb image of U.S. goodwill. The microfarms will enable farmers and families to grow food, feed, biofertilizers and healthy nutritional products on tiny land footprints so they can stay in their communities and not be forced by economics to migrate north.

DHS has responsibility for borders, disaster preparedness and building a resilient nation. The Friendship Bridge project achieves these objectives. Microfarms offer a green algae strategy that provides significant social, health, economic and environmental benefits. When DHS, USDA or another agency funds the Friendship Bridge, they can experience the joy from enabling people to help themselves and their communities instead of living in the shadow of an ugly American fence.

3. How can We Build the Green Friendship Bridge?

Peace microfarms will be optimized for easy and efficient production of various algae cultivars, and especially for spirulina. Spirulina has been eaten by humans for thousands of years, is easy to grow, and benefits from the most research on production and consumption. More algae growers have cultivated spirulina than any other algae specie.

Undernutrition and food insecurity constitute serous public health problems in Mexico and Central America. In some countries, over half the children under five suffer from malnutrition that can be alleviated by locally produced microfarm nutrients. The use of algae, particularly spirulina, as a functional food and nutritional supplement was suggested decades ago by several experts due to it extremely high nutralence – nutrient density, diversity and bioavailability.

Spirulina offers a protein-dense food source with very few calories. Delicious and healthy spirulina foods deliver a superior amino acid profile compared to meat or other vegetables. Spirulina foods contain nutrients with substantially higher biologic-value (due to higher nutralence) than other vegetables or meat.

Spirulina provides essential fats (e.g., gamma-linolenic oleic acids), associated to low content nucleic acids. It has an exceptionally high content of vitamin B and delivers high levels of beta-carotene, iron, calcium and phosphorous. Consumer research shows spirulina's organoleptic properties, taste, sight, smell and touch, makes it attractive as a food or nutrition supplement. Spirulina has exhibited neither acute nor chronic toxicities, making it safe for human consumption. Several companies market spirulina in the U.S. with a GRAS, Generally Recognized as Safe certification from the FDA.

Train trainers

The Friendship Bridge Foundation will put out a call for microfarm trainers in the target countries. Foundation members will train trainers in microfarm construction and operations. Foundation members will help build and operate initial microfarms in each country and communicate lessons learned via YouTube, Skype, Facebook and other social media.

Spirulina – dried and fresh

The Foundation will partner with Antenna Technologies, the World Bank, Spirulina Source, Smart Microfarms and other similar organizations in communicating the value of spirulina and other algae species for food, nutrition, animal feed, biofertilizer, medicines and other bioproducts. The Foundation will link microfarmers and create a Friendship Bridge Cooperative, funded from a small percentage of the microfarmers revenue, to share R&D and additional training.

The Cooperative will become a focus for education, insights and innovation. The Cooperative will provide training for future microfarmers. The Cooperative will provide a stock of selected spirulina cultivars as well as other viable algae species.

The coop, networked to all participating microfarmers, will house educational videos and materials on best-practice methods of cultivation, harvesting and consumption. Microfarmers will coach one another through the network on topical issues. The coop network will include schools where students can view webcams of live microfarming operations. Restaurants and home cooks will showcase their algae recipes, which will increase algae demand and consumption. Universities, hospitals and medical professionals will create studies to validate the substantial nutrition and health benefits from various forms of algae.

Peace microfarm construction

Microfarms can be built in a variety of shapes and sizes to match the geography, climate and target algae species grown.

Algae raceway

Algae PBR

The Friendship Bridge Foundation's role includes communicating the value of spirulina for food, nutrition, animal feed, biofertilizer and medicines. The Foundation would also provide a stock of selected spirulina cultivars with educational videos and materials on best-practice methods of cultivation, harvesting and consumption.

DHS, (USDA, NGO or other donors) would provide funding for the $50,000 cost of each microfarm. Some microfarms may be funded with microloans or other mechanisms.

The project team will source large orders the required materials.

1. Plastic liners for microfarm bottoms and plastic sheets for sides.

2. Paddlewheels or air pumps, harvest filters and other basic equipment.

3. Flasks and beakers to supply a basic on-site lab for inoculates.

Farmers or families will receive their microfarm kit after they have been trained in microfarming and have passed a competency exam. Kits will be nicely packaged in containers so they can be shipped anywhere. Local labor will assemble the microfarm, supplemented where needed, by readily available local materials.

Peace microfarmers will commit to a social entrepreneurial model. In return for the value of the microfarms, recipients, which may be a farmer, family or community, they promise to give half their production to hungry children, pregnant mothers or others suffering from malnutrition. They will be able to sell the second half at fair prices locally.

MicroBio Engineering's prefab algae raceways that are available in many sizes provide excellent microfarm models. John Benemann, CEO of MicroBio Engineering, was recently elected an Algae Ambassador by the algae industry. John Benemann has over 50-years' experience in designing algae projects, including especially wastewater treatment.

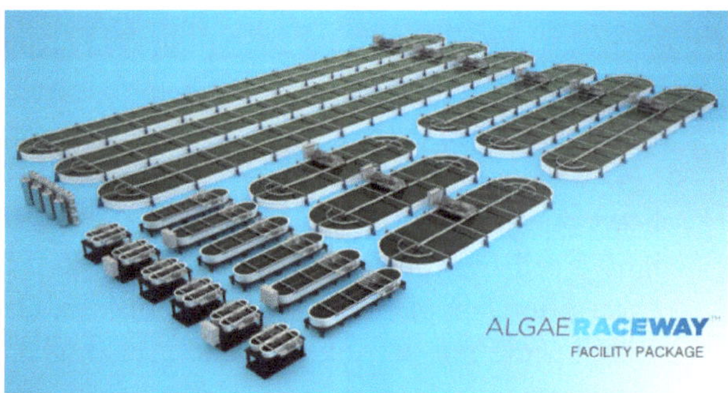

Algae raceways will be delivered as complete packages that include the walls, pre-cut liner, paddle wheels with motors, and extensive monitoring and control systems. All components are specially designed for durability, chemical compatibility, and high performance based on decades of algae industry experience.

Growing food

The primary microfarm inputs required are agricultural fertilizers, water and – optionally – electricity. Some microfarms may use non-potable water such as waste or brine water. Another input, soda or bicarbonate of soda, is typically easy to source locally. Soda may be replaced by solid wood ashes.

The simple growth medium can be made from fertilizers that are usually available in farm communities. Contrary to some expectations, the volume of water required is less than for any other traditional form of agricultural production. With its high productivity and the small amounts of spirulina required per person, the growing surface required is relatively small. The modest microfarm footprint is like an urban garden.

The first harvest is ready within 30 to 44 days after starting operations. Harvest uses a simple filtration of the growth medium. Farmers can harvest daily or several days a week. The filtered rich green biomass is then dried during the day and processed late afternoon.

When the dried mass has been crushed to powder, it can be eaten immediately, or added to traditional foodstuffs. Given its ease of use, spirulina is accepted quickly by mothers when they witness for themselves how their children's health improves. Spirulina tastes best fresh or fresh frozen. With adequate packing, spirulina or spirulina-enriched products can be stored for two to three years. These high-value bioproducts have a long shelf life in local or regional markets.

Spirulina filter harvest and drying – Source: Spirulina Source, Robert Henrikson

Summary

A Green Friendship Bridge composed of 14,000 peace microfarms distributed throughout Mexico and Central America will enable our food insecure neighbors to grow affordable healthy food for their family and community locally. The Friendship Bridge will dramatically advance the cause of freedom and peace.

4. What Foods can Peace Microfarms Grow?

The Green Friendship Bridge project focuses on enabling microfarmers throughout Mexico and Central America to grow food locally, so they do not have to migrate north. The initial training will use spirulina because it is easy to grow, harvest and make into a wide variety of foods.

The next question is: **"What is the range of food products microfarmers can grow?"** The answer is nearly unbelievable, until one understands unique attributes of the oldest and fastest growing plant on the planet, algae.

Any food, fibers or special compounds that can be made from land-based plants can be made from algae because land plants evolved from algae 500 million years ago. Terrestrial plants inherited their DNA from algae and somewhere an algae species resides in a moist habitat that retains the target compounds. Algae offer a much wider array of colors, textures, tastes and compounds than land plants.

Algae foods

Land plant species number less than 300,000, but only a few are useful as food for people. The leading textbook, *Algae* (2nd. Ed, 2008) by James Graham, Lee Wilcox and Linda Graham, estimate algae species number over 10 million. Well over 95% of all their special compounds remain to be discovered, described and cultivated. Algae produce far more compounds than found in land plants because there are so many more species of algae than terrestrial plants and animals. Algae benefit from over 3 billion

more years of adaption and evolution than land plants. Algae have created ingenious survival strategies to maximize their growth and vitality and to repel predators.

Not only are algae far more diverse than terrestrial plants, but algae grow far faster. A farmer growing corn must wait 120 days to harvest the first ounce of protein from the single crop a year. An algae microfarmer may wait 30 days for the inoculate to mature and then harvest daily the rest of the year in warm climates. Each kilo of algae harvested contains 3x the protein of corn.

Corn is a greedy crop and requires substantial cultivation and expensive NPK fertilizers as well as agricultural poisons. Heavy cultivation creates dust clouds and adds to soil loss. Corn consumes 10x more nitrogen than wheat, polluting the atmosphere with considerable NOx (nitrous oxides). Corn, a row crop, magnifies soils losses as wind and water move topsoil, (and fertilizers) quickly and smoothly down the rows.

Dirty harvest for the row crop corn, maize

A single storm, heat spike, drought or pest invasion can destroy a farmer's food grain or vegetable crop. The farmer not only loses a year's worth of field work, but gets zero produce from all the costly inputs. In too many cases, severe crop loss causes farmer bankruptcy.

If a disaster should strike a microfarmer, production can begin again in about a month, before daily harvests begins. Peace microfarms are an excellent disaster relief solution because people typically have abundant microfarm inputs available locally – wastewater and botanical wastes. Microfarms can recycle nutrients from local waste streams to produce healthy and clean foods, biofeeds and biofertilizers, but also clean water. In disaster relieve, clean water may have superior value to the nutritious algae biomass.

Besides superior nutrition, spirulina offers multiple advantages to the environment and those who cultivate it. Spirulina grows quickly and reproduces a growth rate of about 30% a day. Growers can produce 30x more protein each year on each acre or hectare. Spirulina requires 10x less water than other vegetables, 50x less than field crops such as corn and 80x less than growing beef protein.

Growers do not have to expend heavy labor, work with dangerous equipment, be exposed to agricultural poisons or farm in bad weather. Peace microfarms can be designed to enable youth, elderly and even handicapped people to grow food locally.

Algae in food

Consumers eat lots of algae in modern foods as algae ingredients are already integrated throughout our food, feed, cosmetics and medicines. A market basket test at Arizona State University found that nearly 70% of products consumers commonly buy at the supermarket contain compounds sourced from algae. These products include ice cream, functional foods, health foods, dairy, beer, soft drinks, jams, bakery products, soups, sauces, pie fillings, cakes, frostings, colorings, ulcer remedies, digestive aids, eye drops, tooth paste, skin creams and shampoos.

Many dairy products contain carrageenan extracted from red macroalgae, (seaweed) to give creamed soups, sour cream, chocolate milk and cheese a denser consistency. Many dairy products such as milk shakes contain alginic acid that acts as both a stabilizer and emulsifier. Gelatin contains agar that can solidify most foods that come in a liquid form. Agar was first used in China in the 17th century and is now found in hundreds of foods such as pie crusts, pumpkin pie filling, breads, pastries and flavored gelatin.

Carrageenan in red algae Alginic acid in kelp

Most people outside of Asia do not eat algae directly but enjoy the products made from algae components that include: algae flour in lieu of wheat, corn or soy flour; algae oils that are healthier and less fattening than food grain oils, and algae nutrients such as essential vitamins, minerals, trace elements and Omega 3 fatty acids.

Algae supply high-protein, low-fat, nutritious, healthy and delicious human foods. Algae provide more vitamins, minerals and nutrients than land plants because their cell size is so tiny, 5 to 10 microns, a small fraction of terrestrial plant cells. Small cell size creates massive surface area for nutrient absorbtion and adsorption. Adsorption is the process whereby some elements and molecules cling to, (chelate with) the outside of the cell. Algae consumers receive the benefits of all algae nutrients because the tiny cell size makes the nutrients highly bioabsorbable.

Algae provide more nutralence than any other food on earth. Nutralence includes nutrient density, nutrient diversity and biosorption, (uptake in the stomach). Terrestrial plants are extremely limited in nutrient density due to cell size and plant composition. Many plants provide "hidden hunger" where the consumer eats lots of calories but gets only a few nutrients per bite.

Nutrient diversity is restricted in land plants by the reach of their roots and nutrient carrying capacity. If specific nutrients, vitamins or minerals are not present and absorbable in the soil, the plant often grows but without important nutrients. Nutrient deficiency amplifies hidden hunger. Many vegetables in supermarkets such as tomatoes have only a fraction of the nutrients found 30 years ago because they are grown on worn-out soil.

Lots of produce suffers from nutrient dilution. Farmers over fertilize, especially with nitrogen, to "pump up the produce." When the consumer buys the big and heavy produce, most the extra weight comes from water, which dilutes the nutrients in each bite. Since water weighs about 8.3 pounds per gallon, water weight adds up quickly because farmers are paid by produce weight, combined with appearance and size. Fruits such as watermelon, strawberries, grapefruit, cantaloupe and peaches contain over 90%

water. Cucumber, lettuce, zucchini, radish, eggplant, tomato and cabbage contain over 92% water.

It may seem improbable that tiny algae cells can provide sufficient vitamin A, iodine, iron, zinc and other nutrients, even when the local diet does not. Typically, these critical trace elements exist in the local water but only in extremely weak dilution. People, especially children, are unable to drink enough water to acquire sufficient iodine. In many ecosystems, little fresh water is available for drinking. Algae's secret to high nutralence stems from its ability to bioaccumulate nutrients in water at 1,000 times ambient levels. This means that even when some nutrients, minerals or vitamins may be lacking in human diets, algae concentrate those nutrients in the green biomass.

Algae do not provide a full solution for malnutrition because the biomass delivers very few calories. However, calories are cheap to produce and easy to grow. One smart malnutrition strategy uses algae foods made from spirulina to restore essential nutrients and algae biofertilizer to enhance the growth of nut trees or peanuts that provide plenty of calories.

Algae as food

Macroalgae or sea vegetables have been eaten directly in Asia since at least 600 B.C. A list of common edible macroalgae shows a wide range of sea vegetables. Sea vegetable are known as the "marine medicinal food" because they contain many health-promoting molecules and materials, such as dietary fiber, omega-3 fatty acids, essential amino acids, and vitamins A, B, C, and E. Sea vegetables contain considerable protein, a few lipids and large amounts of dietary fiber. Dietary fiber promotes digestion when passing through the gastrointestinal tract. This function may reduce the risk of colorectal cancers, reduction of bowel inflammation and abdominal disorders and facilitate bowel movements.

Seaweed, similar to other algae species, has low caloric content and high dietary fiber, which can help control weight gain. Consumers feel fuller quicker as the food expands in the stomach and eat less. Microfarmers along sea coasts can grow macroalgae. In addition, various microalgae can provide nutrients like macroalgae.

Microalgae such as spirulina provide an excellent source of foods and food ingredients such as lipids, proteins, polysaccharides, phenolics, carotenoids. Spirulina offers rich protein, about 60% by weight, which is 2 ½ times more protein per kilo than red meat. It also contains all the essential amino acids, and 10 of the 12 non-essential amino acids, along with a potent array of other beneficial nutrients.

Highly digestible protein 83 - 90 % digestible.	B vitamins (including exceptionally high B-12), K, and other vitamins.	Phytopigments (phycocyanin, chlorophyll, and carotenoids).	Minerals, Ca, Fe, Mg, K, Zn
Vitamin E, four times as much vitamin B12 as raw liver.	Best source of gamma-linolenic acid an important fatty acid for heart and joint health.	Essential fatty acids, e.g. sulfolipids. protect against HIV infection of T-helper cells.	Metallo-thionine proteins chelate heavy radioactive isotopes)
Naturally rich in iodine.	Low icarbo-hydrates, 5-20%.	Similar P, Ca and Mg to cow's milk.	Eighteen amino acids.

Spirulina's impressive nutralence package

Spirulina's protein efficiency ratio is very high, meaning the body efficiently uses the amino acids. Medical research reinforces that spirulina's biosorption by the body is among the highest of any foods. Field studies show that children who received a spirulina supplement daily five days a week for two months had better nutritional status and improved intellectual status compared to those who did not. Web MD posts ratings on vitamins and supplements. Spirulina received 5-star ratings on effectiveness, ease of use and satisfaction. NASA and The European Space Agency are researching how to use spirulina in astronauts' diets on a Mars mission.

Peace microfarms can produce healthier foods that deliver high nutralence with colorful and tasty forms. Spirulina foods provide superior nutrition and have decades of history with chefs and household cooks. Fresh, frozen or dried into flour, spirulina foods may be protein bars, burgers, drinks, cakes, ice cream or cookies. Only one factor limits algae cooks – imagination!

5. What are Social Benefits for the Green Friendship Bridge?

Peace microfarms will enable farmers and families to grow algae-based food, feed, biofertilizers and healthy nutritional products locally on tiny non-cropland footprints so they can stay in their homes and not be forced by economics to migrate to feed their families.

Microfarmers south of the U.S. border are likely to choose to grow spirulina because this 3-billion-year old plant is indigenous to the region. Indigenous spirulina typically outperforms cultures obtained from algae libraries or institutions. The local spirulina stain has invested eons in adapting to the vulgarities of the local microclimate.

Desert-adapted species thrive in normal years and survive when their pond habitats evaporate. Rather than die when the weather goes bad, as land plants do, algae cells simply go into a dormant state. Algae can survive on rocks as hot as 70° C, (160° F). In this dormant condition, the naturally blue-green algae turn a frosty white cake and develop a sweet flavor. Intense heat transforms its 70% protein structure into polysaccharide sugars.

Joan Myers, a phenomenal photographer for National Geographic documents extreme environments such as ice floes and volcanoes. Her latest book, *Fire and Ice* is amazing. Joan shared a fascinating story.

She and a scientist were pulling cores from below the snow and ice sheet in the 17-million-year-old Beacon Valley in Antarctica. When they returned to the lab, they removed a million-year-old rock and cracked it open. What did they find? Dormant blue-green algae. When they added water, the algae came to life.

Spirulina may have a Biblical history too. Prior Aglae101 posts suggest that the "manna" of the wandering Israelites in the *Bible* may have been spirulina and lichen, an alga - fungi symbiant. The product appeared miraculously each morning on rocks with the dew. Manna was described as tasting "like wafers made with honey." This is consistent with the taste of spirulina scrapped off hot rocks, (that have cooled).

Spirulina thrives in very warm waters of 32 to 45° C, (approximately 85 to 112 ° F), and has even survived in temperatures of 60 ° C, (140 ° F). Growers at high altitudes may find their cultures are productive possibly 6 – 8 months of the year. Some growers use greenhouses to extend the growing season. Others use LED grow lights and water heaters to produce year-round.

The fresh-water lakes, ponds and commercial cultures spirulina favors are quite alkaline, in the range of 8 to 11 pH. The high alkalinity diminishes competition from other microorganisms. Fresh water spirulina can adapt to brine, (salty) and even sea water. Some microfarmers use wastewater where the algae recover and recycle the waste nutrients. These growers may target animal feed or biofertilizer with their production because food-grade algae must have near-zero contaminants.

Spirulina's unique ability to grow in hot and alkaline environments ensures its hygienic status. Other contaminating microorganisms cannot survive in the highly alkaline culture to compete with spirulina for nutrient and photon, (solar) resources. Spirulina is one of the cleanest, most naturally sterile foods found in nature because the alkalinity is off-putting to potential contaminating microorganisms.

Shelf life and nutritional retention are critical for foods. Most plant and animal foods deteriorate very quickly at high temperatures. Shrimp, for example, offer a highly dense nutrient food package, largely because they are what they eat: algae. Both the shrimp meat and nutrients sour within minutes in the sun. Spirulina's adaption to heat allows the cells to go dormant when heat stress occurs so it can regenerate and begin quickly propagating again when good growing conditions return. Spirulina biomass retains its nutritional value when subject to high temperatures during growing, harvest, processing and storage.

Spirulina cells are extremely large for a single-celled organism, attaining sizes of 0.5 millimeters in length. This is about 100 times the size of most other algae. Some individual spirulina cells are visible to the naked eye but studying a culture requires a microscope.

Spirulina spirals linked together

Spirulina's prolific cellular reproductive capacity and their proclivity to adhere and form spiral colonies makes spirulina a large and easily harvested green biomass. Indigenous people harvested spirulina using baskets to sweep the biomass off the surface of the water. Today, microfarmers typically use a fine mesh sieve to filter the spirals out of the water.

Spirulina is a "nuclear plant," on the developmental crossroad between plants and animals. It is considered above plants because it does not have the hard-cellulose membranes characteristic of plant cells. Spirulina does not have a well-defined nucleus, hence its classification as a cyanobacteria.

Spirulina's metabolic system is typical of plant life forms based on photosynthesis. Spirulina produces direct food energy like other plants utilizing sunlight and chlorophyll. Spirulina embodies the simplest form of life. In contrast, other algae such as chlorella have developed the hard, largely indigestible walls characteristic of plants.

Farmers may choose to grow spirulina, another algae species or some local indigenous algae adapted to the specific microclimate. A 2015 review article on the nutritional value of Australian microalgae for human health found that Australian native microalgal species Scenedesmus sp., Nannochloropsis sp., Dunaliella sp., and a chlorophytic polyculture have great potential as multi-nutrient human health supplements. These algae species can also be found in Mexico and Central America where growing conditions are similar. Global research shows that microfarmers have many algae species they may choose to grow, each offering unique target compounds.

Most microfarmers begin growing spirulina because decades of experience are available on optimal growing, harvesting and making valuable bioproducts.

Social benefits

The visual image of green growing systems supporting families and community trumps an ugly border wall. The border wall is an expensive, passive edifice that does not align with U.S. values. The wall is an embarrassment for many Americans. It creates a porous barrier to illegal immigrants who can go over, under, around and through at various points.

Immigrant dolls and a Peace microfarm

Peace microfarms provide a beautiful green image of self-sufficiency and vibrancy. Microfarms are active, productive growing systems that support farmers, families and communities. Peace microfarms can be sited on tiny non-cropland footprints such as back yards, rooftops, parking lots, train right-of-ways, rocky areas, wasteland and deserts.

Microfarms give growers the liberty to produce healthy and delicious nutrients and foods for their families and communities. Growers have the freedom to produce a wide range of valuable bioproducts including healthy omega-3 fatty acids, nutraceuticals and cosmeceuticals. Other growers may produce animal feeds that improve the health, coats and vitality of their animals. Top stallion owners feed omega-3 supplements to their sires to increase sperm production and improve the odds for successful breeding.

The use of algae for animal feed is not new. Julius Caesar's armies fed algae to their horses to improve the sheen in their coats as well as their stamina. Caesar's horse soldiers found that algae improved their horses' night vision as well as recovery from injury. The women in Caesar's court used a red pigment from an algae-fungi symbiont, lichen, for rouge on their cheeks.

Location independence

Many areas are not suitable for farming due to geography, soils or climate. Microfarmers can grow food nearly anywhere there is sunshine. Local food production enables farmers to stay in their community and not be forced to migrate. Advanced growers can supplement solar energy with high-efficiency LED lighting using controlled environment agriculture.

Microfarms, also called green solar gardens, provide an excellent opportunity for training people throughout the region in sustainable farming practices. Microfarms are learning environments where lateral learning thrives as microfarmers share their insights and experience.

Microfarms can learn to produce freedom foods that use no or minimal fossil resources including fertile soil, fresh water, fossil fuels, chemical fertilizers or agriculture poisons. Freedom Foods are sustainable, leave the environmental footprint of a butterfly and preserve valuable natural resources for future generations.

Freedom foods reinvent our food supply from the foundation of the food chain to liberate consumers to make smart choices for healthier, delicious food. Food grown low on the food chain free food producers from the heavy consumption, waste and pollution caused by modern industrial foods. Consumers do not have free choice today because Freedom Foods are not widely available. Peace microfarms will create a revolution to transform the food supply using abundance methods. Abundance production methods free growers from fossil resources by using plentiful resources that will not run out – sunshine, CO_2, sterilized waste stream nutrients and brine or ocean water. In many areas in Mexico and Central America, plentiful brine water is located so near the soil surface it can be extracted by a foot pump.

Youth unemployment is high in many regions. Peace microfarms do not require heavy labor, heavy machinery or stamina. Therefore, microfarms can be operated by young people, the handicapped and the elderly to grow heathy food. Microfarm training is immediately transferable to traditional forms of agriculture, which make microfarms an excellent training environment. Some microfarmers expand production beyond algae to microgreens, herbs and hydroponic vegetables. Others expand their systems to grow fish in aquaculture systems where algae provide biofeed for shell or fin fish.

Social benefits summary

The Green Friendship Bridge project benefits from the ability of spirulina and other algae species to grow quickly in microfarms. Peace microfarms provide a far superior picture compared with an ugly border wall. Microfarms provide an attractive picture of sustainable self-sufficiency that brings joy and vitality to families and communities.

Peace microfarms may serve as learning environments for sustainable food production. The Friendship Bridge Cooperative that networks grower can provide strong lateral learning. Champions may create training programs at local schools and colleges to expand the knowledge about local food production.

6. What are the Green Friendship Bridge Health Benefits?

The many microfarm health benefits may eclipse the economics of job creation and local food production. Farmers may choose to grow spirulina, chlorella or a local indigenous alga adapted to the specific microclimate. Most microfarmers begin producing spirulina because it is the easiest to grow and is indigenous to the region.

Why spirulina?

Spirulina grows naturally in mineral-rich alkaline lakes which can be found on every continent, often near volcanoes. The largest natural stands of spirulina today can be found at Lake Texcoco in Mexico, around Lake Chad in Central Africa and along the Great Rift Valley lakes in east Africa where the oldest human fossils, e.g. "Lucy," have been found.

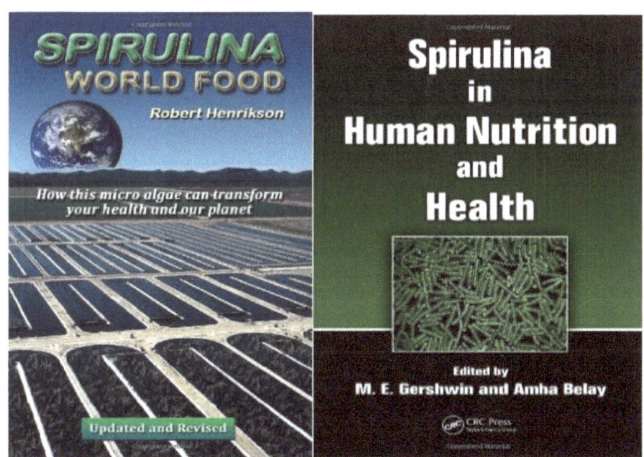

Two of the best books on spirulina: Robert Henrikson and Gershwin and Belay.

Many spirulina species have been found globally, but two that are indigenous to California, Mexico and Mesoamerica are *spirulina platensis* and *spirulina maxima*. Each has been widely cultivated and studied extensively due to their high nutritional and therapeutic values.

In Mexico and Central America, spirulina grows spontaneously in ponds and lakes. It thrives in fresh, brine and salt water. Many climates in Mexico and Central America can grow spirulina year- round.

Spirulina is typically eaten locally fresh or dried. Solar drying it into a powder creates a flour similar to food grains that can be made into bread, tortillas, crepes or cakes. Fresh spirulina can be eaten directly without any processing or cooking, eliminating costly energy consumption.

Spirulina has a colorful history as a nutritional food source for the Aztecs in Mexico. One of Cortés' soldiers described how local Aztec women harvested spirulina from Lake Texcoco and sold spirulina cakes in the local market. The Aztecs called it Tecuitlatl, which means the stone's excrement. French researchers rediscovered abundant spirulina in the lake during the 1960s and the industry has flourished since.

Spirulina served as a food in Chad, as far back as the 9th century Kanem Empire. Today it is dried into cakes called Dihe, which are made into soups, stews, breads and cookies and sold fresh in local markets. The Spirulina is harvested from small lakes and ponds around Lake Chad using methods that date back centuries.

Spirulina cakes for sale near Lake Chad

Today Spirulina is consumed by millions of people all over the world due to strong health benefits and nutritive value. The Great Algae Space Race in the 1950s and 60s reignited demand for spirulina. Both the Soviet Space Program and NASA proposed that Spirulina could be grown in space and used by astronauts for food, nutritional supplements and reclaiming wastewater. Recent NASA and European Space Agency research on supporting astronaut travel to Mars has rekindled spirulina for space flights.

The UN-Food and Agriculture Organization, (FAO) recommends both national governments and inter-governmental organizations to re-evaluate the potential of Spirulina to fulfill both their own food security needs as well as a tool for their overseas development emergency response efforts.

The World Health Organization, (WHO), calls spirulina "An interesting food for multiple reasons, rich in iron and protein, and can be administered to children without any risk. We at WHO consider it a very suitable food." WHO currently sponsors small microfarms in Kenya, Iraq, Republic of the Congo, Dominican Republic/Haiti, Peru and Columbia. Spirulina was declared by the United Nations World Food Conference of 1974 as the "best food for the future."

Spirulina nutrition

Spirulina, a cyanobacteria, is typically referred to as blue-green algae. Spirulina, like terrestrial plants, can produce energy out of sunlight, via photosynthesis. Plants use photon energy to transform carbon dioxide and water into simple plant sugar, (glucose) and oxygen.

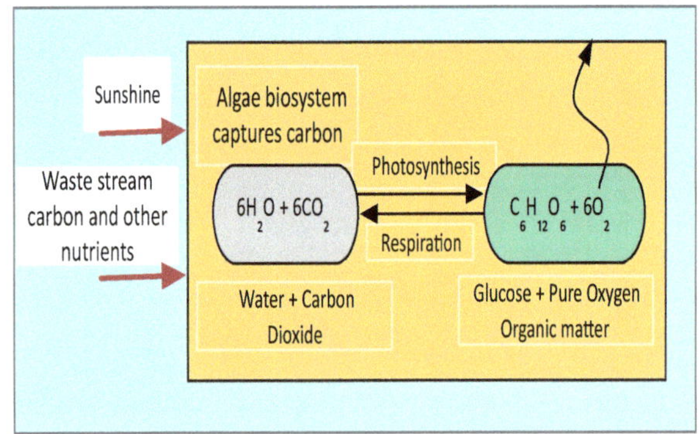

The miraculous power of photosynthesis

The rich green biomass has the highest nutralence – nutrient density, nutrient diversity and bioavailability – of any food on earth. Spirulina packs in protein, vitamins, minerals, carotenoids, and antioxidants that can help protect cells from damage. Spirulina contains some 60 substances

beneficial to the human organism, including all essential amino acids, a broad variety of minerals and vitamins, carotenoids and antioxidants. It contains nutrients, including B-complex vitamins, beta-carotene, vitamin E, manganese, zinc, copper, iron, selenium, and gamma linolenic acid (an essential fatty acid).

Spirulina grows in microscopic spirals, which tend to stick together, making it easy to harvest. It has an intense blue-green color, but a relatively mild taste. The FDA allows manufacturers to use Spirulina as a color additive in candy and other packaged foods. Spirulina may be marketed in the U.S. as a food supplement and has GRAS status (Generally Accepted as Safe) from the FDA.

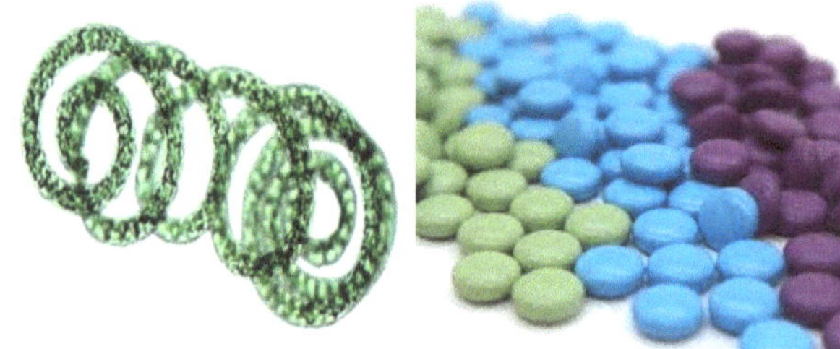

Spirulina's spirals and blue and green pigments

A single tablespoon, (7 grams) of dried spirulina powder contains:

- Protein: 4 grams, Vitamin B1 (Thiamin): 11% of the RDA.

- Vitamin B2 (Riboflavin): 15% of the RDA, Vitamin B3 (Niacin): 4% of the RDA.

- Copper: 21% of the RDA, Iron: 11% of the RDA.

It also contains magnesium, potassium and manganese, and small amounts of almost every other micronutrient we need. The tablespoon delivers only 20 calories and 1.7 grams of digestible carbohydrate.

A tablespoon of spirulina contains a small amount of fat (around 1 gram), including both omega-6 and omega-3 fatty acids in about a 1.5:1 ratio. The quality of the protein in spirulina is considered excellent, comparable to eggs and contains all the essential amino acids. A quarter pound spirulina vegie burger delivers 2 ½ times the protein of beef and more than twice the protein of soy bean.

Health benefits

Many families are food insecure and do not get sufficient nutrients. In El Salvador, Guatemala, Honduras, and Nicaragua, over 50% of children under five are malnourished. Half of Mexico's children live in poverty. World Vision released a report showing 36% of Mexican children are malnourished. Currently, 1.5 million children suffer from chronic malnutrition in Mexico; while two million children under five are anemic. Anemia occurs when the body does not make enough red blood cells. Symptoms include fatigue, weakness, pale or yellowish skin, irregular heartbeats, shortness of breath, dizziness or lightheadedness, chest pain and headache.

Protein-energy malnutrition, (PEM) causes stunting, slowing of linear growth. Behavioral changes occur such as irritability, apathy, decreased social responsiveness, anxiety, and attention deficits that lead to problems in school. Unfortunately, the early childhood effects of malnutrition, once they are expressed, are irreversible.

Clinical signs and symptoms of micronutrient deficiencies include the following.

- **Iron** - Fatigue, anemia, decreased cognitive function, headache, glossitis, and nail changes.

- **Iodine** - Goiter, developmental delay, and mental retardation.

- **Vitamin D** - Poor growth, rickets, and hypocalcemia.

- **Vitamin A** - Night blindness, xerophthalmia, poor growth, and hair changes.

- **Folate** - Glossitis, anemia, (megaloblastic), and neural tube defects (in fetuses of women without folate supplementation).

- **Zinc** - Anemia, dwarfism, hepatosplenomegaly, hyperpigmentation and hypogonadism, acrodermatitis enteropathica, diminished immune response and poor wound healing.

A single microfarm can provide these critical nutrients for several families or for an entire community. Local microfarms can eliminate malnutrition.

Malnutrition in children

Pregnant mothers who get insufficient nutrients from their diet, especially folic acid, often deliver low birthweight babies, many of whom become stunted and intellectually challenged. The primary nutrient deficiency in pregnant mothers that lead to labor death and low birthweight babies are iron Deficiency Anemia, Vitamin A and Iodine deficiency. A local microfarm can provide sufficient nutrients to support healthy mothers and their babies.

Global warming amplifies water shortages that are addressed with deeper wells. Experience shows that deeper wells tend to increase levels of heavy metal poisons including especially iron, lead, mercury and arsenic. Eating algae foods allows the body to bioabsorb the tiny algae cells that chelate with heavy metals which are then passed out of the body in the urine. In regions plagued with heavy metals in drinking water, the ability of spirulina to detox heavy metal poisoning can save children, adults and the elderly.

Pesticide pollution imposes terrible illnesses on pregnant mothers, fetuses and young children. Recent research shows a connection between pesticide exposure by pregnant mothers and autism spectrum disorders in children. Pesticides cause short-term impacts such as headaches and nausea to chronic impacts like cancer, reproductive harm, and endocrine disruption.

People exposed to these poisons in crop fields, in nearby towns and even pesticide residuals on produce may experience acute dangers such as nerve, skin, and eye irritation and damage, headaches, dizziness, nausea, fatigue, and systemic poisoning.

Only about 1% of agricultural poisons are absorbed by the pest targets. Some of the remainder escapes the field and pollutes local communities. Substantial residuals may remain on produce even after washing. Microfarms produce high-quality food without pesticide. Additional research suggests that spirulina eaten normally can chelate with the poison molecules, attach to heavy metals, which allows the body to flush the poisons naturally.

A FAO review of spirulina as food for humans and domestic animals details the appropriateness of spirulina as a nutritional supplement in humanitarian emergencies. In addition to the health issues addressed above, microfarms producing spirulina offer additional health benefits.

- **Immune support** – spirulina increases production of antibodies, infection-fighting proteins, and other cells that improve immunity and help ward off infection and chronic illnesses, such as heart disease and cancer.

- **Protein supplement** – amino acids make up 62% of spirulina. Because it is a rich source of protein and other nutrients, spirulina has been used as a nutritional supplement.

- **Allergic Reactions** –studies suggest that spirulina may protect against allergic reactions by stopping the release of histamines, substances that contribute to allergy symptoms, such as a runny nose, watery eyes, hives and soft-tissue swelling.

- **Antibiotic-related Illnesses** – Although antibiotics destroy unwanted organisms in the body, they may also kill "good" bacteria called probiotics, such as *Lactobacillus acidophilus*. This can cause diarrhea. In test tubes, spirulina has boosted the growth of *L. acidophilus* and other probiotics.

- **Infection** – Studies suggest that spirulina has activity against herpes, influenza, and HIV. Several recent publications reported that HIV/AIDS patients recovered faster with spirulina.

- **Oral cancer** – in a placebo-controlled study, taking spirulina seemed to reduce a precancerous lesion known as leukoplasia in people who chewed tobacco. Lesions were more likely to go away in the spirulina group than in the placebo group.

- **Liver disorders** – Preliminary evidence suggests that spirulina may help protect against liver damage and cirrhosis (liver failure) in people with chronic hepatitis.

- **Eye Diseases** – Spirulina contains a high concentration of zeaxanthin, an important nutrient linked to eye health. Spirulina may help reduce the risk of cataracts and age-related macular degeneration.

Additional research is needed to validate the multiple ways spirulina nutrients support human and animal health.

Algae prevent disease

Market research shows that people strongly prefer following the advice of Hippocrates: "*Let food be thy medicine in the medicine be thy food.*" Algae already support our global food system as useful ingredients, valuable compounds for functional foods, and in some cases, algae food.

Algae offer novel biosolutions. Algae are photoautotrophic cell factories that provide an efficient means of converting solar energy into biomass composed of fatty acids, lipids, vitamins, carbohydrates, antibiotics, antioxidants, proteins and bioactive compounds that can battle disease.

Algae compounds prevent disease by providing the essential nutrients for sustained health and vitality. Algae contain high multiples of the nutrients that cause the major nutrient deficiencies globally. Algae contain several times more beta-carotene, (provitamin A) than other foods. Algae are rich in antioxidant vitamins, (C and E), in concentrations far higher than any land plants. Vitamin C provides protection against immune system deficiencies, CHD, prenatal health problems, eye disease, and skin wrinkling. Vitamin E moderates neurological problems due to poor nerve conduction and anemia due to oxidative damage to red blood cells. Algae are a good source of all seven B vitamins. Algae offer a unique as a plant source of vitamin B12.

What are the Green Friendship Bridge Health Benefits?

Algae medical treatments

Algae offer therapeutic protection or treatment for many diseases. Peer-reviewed scientific research provides algae-based medical solutions for the following health challenges.

Deficiencies	Major organs	Diseases
Vitamins	Brain	Blood pressure
Minerals	Eyes	Hyperlipidemia
Elements	Heart	Bleeding gums
Antioxidants	Lungs	Infections
Hormones	Kidneys	Inflammation
Disorders	Skin, hair, nails	Cancers
Mood	Liver	Immune
Anxiety	Blood	Viral infection
Psychotic	Pancreas	Infections
Personality	Hypothalamus	Injuries
Sexual	Pituitary	Diarrhea
Development	Thyroid	Diabetes
Brain	Nerves	Obesity

Algae prevent or remediate nutrient deficiencies, which inflict pain and development disorders on nearly half of the world's people. Algae compounds offer medical treatments to restore healthy functioning to major organs and major body systems. Algae have therapeutic properties that improve health and prevent disease that are not found in terrestrial plants. Algae evolved in incredibly harsh environments and developed hundreds of bioactive compounds that defend against predators and disease. Land plants invest their energy in roots and physical structure. Algae do not.

Health benefits summary

The Green Friendship Bridge project leverages the substantial nutrition package delivered by spirulina and other algae species to eliminate childhood, (and adult) malnutrition. In addition, local peace microfarms can support the nutrition of pregnant mothers and eliminate the severe problem of low birthweight babies caused by maternal malnutrition.

Additional research will surely discover new avenues where spirulina and other algae species provide sound solutions to health challenges. The good news is that locally grown spirulina offers superior nutrition with a great constellation of health advantages at a low cost – safely.

We need to begin building peace microfarms NOW!

7. What are Environmental Benefits for the Green Friendship Bridge?

In 1990, 4.5 million Mexicans lived in the U.S. By 2000, the number more than doubled to 9.75 million, and in 2008 it peaked at 12.7 million. This migration is not because so many millions of people are eager to leave their families behind in order to chase some dream in the U.S. Economic policies, in particular the 1994 North American Free Trade Agreement, (NAFTA), created this massive immigration by destroying Mexico's economy.

Immigrants going over the fence

U.S. farm policy, namely subsidies, created artificially low prices for food grain products, corn oil and corn sugars.

Over 1.5 million Mexican farmers were forced to leave their land because they could not compete with subsidized U.S. foods.

Subsidized U.S. corn pushed prices in Mexico down by more than 50%, but corn was not the only problem. Mexico imported 30,000 tons of pork in 1995, the year NAFTA took effect. By 2010, pork imports from the U.S. had grown over 25 times, to 811,000 tons. As a result, pork prices received by Mexican producers dropped 56%. Farmer margins a slim. U.S. farmers could not survive a 50+% drop in crop or meat prices.

Thousands of Mexican farmers, large and small, lost their farms to bankruptcy due to U.S. farm policy. When their crops and animal sales could not pay for their increasingly costly agricultural inputs, farmers were forced into bankruptcy.

Able-bodied people had no choice but to move to the U.S. to work because they could not get a fair price for their food grains or meat products at home. They had to leave their land, their homes and move north. They had no alternative, if they wanted to survive. In rural areas such as Oaxaca Mexico, some towns became depopulated. Vibrant towns transformed into tiny communities of the very old and very young.

Food riot in Mexico

When Mexican meat and corn producers were driven from their farms market by U.S. imports, the Mexican economy was left vulnerable to price changes dictated by U.S. agribusiness or policy. When the U.S. modified its corn policy to encourage ethanol, half of U.S. corn production was burned for fuel. The U.S. had supplied over half the world's corn in export but millions of tons were burned to fuel big American cars. Predictably, ethanol production from corn ignited food shortages in the U.S. and around the world, which led to food riots in Mexico.

U.S. ethanol subsidies for corn created a ripple effect around the world. When the price of corn tortillas, a pillar of the Mexican diet, quadrupled in late 2006, people took to the streets. The "tortilla riots" were the first in a series of over 50 food riots that hit over 30 countries as the cost of agricultural commodities, including especially food grains, reached all-time highs.

The image of Americans burning food to make fuel for cars was and is atrocious. The incredibly foolish U.S. biofuel policy motivated *BioWar I, Why Battles over Food and Fuel Lead to World Hunger.* Burning food throughout the history of civilization has been an uncivilized act of war

that imposed terrible punishment and hunger on the enemy. The Energy Policy Act signed by President George Bush in 2005 made the U.S. the **first society in history to burn its own food**. Because of the Act, 28 million poor and hungry Americans on food support doubled, while food prices surged in the U.S. and globally.

BioWar I follows the money trail to document how a few large agribusiness companies, most notably ADM, profited immensely from the huge ethanol subsidies that resulted in global food riots. *BioWar I* has been used by lobbyists to roll back the catastrophic subsidies for corn ethanol.

The Environmental Working Group reported that U.S. corn subsidies totaled $94.3 billion from 1995-2014, even more than the cost of Trump's Wall. The U.S. government energy policy still supports ethanol. Iowa State University reported in 2015 that 39% of the U.S. corn crop is being diverted to make ethanol. The U.S. Department of Homeland Security should consider joining the World Trade Organization where several countries, including Mexico and Canada, that are suing to end U.S. crop subsidies.

The Renewable Fuel Standard, (RFS) supporting the corn ethanol tax imposes a wealth transfer tax from non-ethanol-producing states to those that make the fuel. By requiring the consumption of fuel that is more expensive than gasoline on an energy-equivalent basis, Congress has imposed a de facto regressive fuel tax on American motorists.

The arguments for corn ethanol consumption are regularly couched in terms of helping rural communities, as well as promoting "energy independence." Research has consistently shown that neither of those to claims are true. Since 2007, the RFS, which requires fuel retailers to blend corn ethanol into the gasoline they sell, has saddled American motorists with more than $10 billion per year in extra fuel costs, above what they would have paid if they had purchased gasoline alone. Adding substantial costs to inefficient fuels hurts, not helps, rural communities. Subsidizing corn ethanol production retards growth in truly green alternative energy production that does support U.S. energy independence.

Additional subsidies for corn ethanol also litter the tax code – including tax breaks for biodiesel and blender pumps, which dispense higher blends of ethanol. DOE programs and other subsidies scattered throughout the federal government, such as the RFS, foolishly mandate the use of corn ethanol.

Local production

Peace microfarms can produce excellent food, feed and other bioproducts locally. Farmers' markets provide a good model for microfarm to table sales. "Fresh and local" are strong drivers for consumers interested in healthy food choices. Local sales create a competitive advantage for each microfarmer, assuming their markets for fresh product does not overlap.

Robert Henrikson's field research found that big spirulina producers get only about 10% of the retail price selling bulk spirulina in quantity to manufacturers. A microfarmer may capture 35% of the retail price when they sell spirulina tablets, bottled drinks, package protein bars or market branded products and through the typical retail distribution system. Channel members consume 65% of the product value. When microfarmers sell direct to customers in the local community, fresh, frozen or dried, they can capture 100% of the retail value.

Small producers can sell fresh algae locally. Fresh may be kept refrigerated for about 4 days. Frozen can be kept much longer. Fresh or frozen spirulina typically sells for 2x or 3x the value of dried product. Fresh spirulina offers many other advantages including no time or energy required for drying or making specialty products such as pasta. Fresh spirulina has a neutral, fresh taste and can be added to just about any food or drink to improve nutralence. Fresh spirulina remains a specialty with local production because the self-life is far too short for distant producers.

Many French spirulina growers sell their entire production each year. Many can only grow their spirulina during the warmer months in France. Some growers produce algae for a living, but most supplement their income with their spirulina microfarm.

Family profit

Peace microfarms grow microcrops that produce

Source: Spirulinasource.com

Experience in France

The Federation des Spiruliniers de France offers an excellent model for networked microfarmers. Jean-Paul Jourdan published his manual "Cultivez Votre Spiruline," (Grow Your Own Spirulina) in 2002. Gilles Planchon published "La Spiruline Pour Tous," ("Spirulina for Everybody") in 2009, an easy-to-read manual (in French) for growing spirulina.

A spirulina school was established at the CFPPA Center in Hyères in 2005. Hyères is an agricultural campus. Jean-Paul Jourdan became a professor of spirulina culture, engaging more people to join this community and training entrepreneurs to grow their own algae business. The number of microfarmers grew and by 2008 the Fédération des Spiruliniers was organized as an association with 80 members. Collectively, they agreed on good business practices and guidelines for quality control. In 2011 work began on a Federation Charter, with quality control standards and good manufacturing practices. One goal is to coordinate food standards with government agencies on regulatory issues as they arise.

healthy protein 30 to 50 times faster than field crops such as corn. After about 30 days of growing the inoculate, a microfarmer can harvest about 30% of the biomass daily, or choose to harvest a higher percentage every two days during sunny weather. Growers can produce algae food and algae bioproducts year-round in many regions of Mexico and Central America.

Microfarms enable farmers and families to make enough money to stay on their land. These farms will not make them rich, but they will have the means to provide healthy food for their family and food to sell in their community.

Rural areas especially suffer from high unemployment. Youth unemployment in Central America exceeds 30% in many regions. A modest microfarm may employ two people and possibly more. One person may focus on growing and harvesting algae. A second might take the food or bioproducts to market.

If the microfarmer grows spirulina, the grower may choose to dry the product or sell it fresh locally. Fresh or frozen spirulina can be eaten directly without any processing or cooking.

Algae microfarm

Example: 50 m² (544 ft²) microfarm, (surface area)

About 3 m (10 ft.) by 17 m (56 ft.)
Volume about 4,000 gallons at 15 cm depth.

This microfarm yields about 135 kg /yr. of spirulina.

Antenna research shows that an 8-week spirulina treatment with 100 g (total) resolves childhood malnutrition. Therefore, each microfarms can deliver enough spirulina to cure **1,350 children** and/or pregnant mothers from the curse of malnutrition.

If the 14,000 peace microfarms in the Green Friendship Bridge project averaged 135 kg of spirulina a year, the microfarms could cure over 19 million children from malnutrition. That is a worthy goal because it helps not only the kids, our next generation, but their families, schools, medical facilities and communities. Stronger kids grow up to be better citizens and to be strong contributors to local economic prosperity.

Microfarmers are expected to give half of their algae production to resolve local malnutrition. New microfarm designs combined with the smart monitoring and growers' network will more than double the 135 kg /yr. of spirulina. The remaining production will create earnings to support the family and sustain motivation in microfarm production.

As growers learn innovative production techniques, microfarm productivity will rise to benefit more people in the community, as well as the growers. Experience will also broaden the range of bioproducts grown, which will enhance expansion opportunities and profitability.

Many communities have scarce potable water, but have abundant wastewater. Where wastewater is not available, peace microfarms can produce effectively with brackish, brine or even more saline ocean water. Over half the water stored on the planet is brine water that is too salty to drink. Many algae species, including spirulina, thrive when grown in brine water.

Wastewater remediation

Global communities have used algae to clean wastewater for over 70 years. Organic and inorganic substances released into the environment from domestic, agricultural and industrial activities pollute water. Primary wastewater treatment processes eliminate the easily settled materials and oxidize the organic material. The clean effluent is discharged safely into natural water bodies.

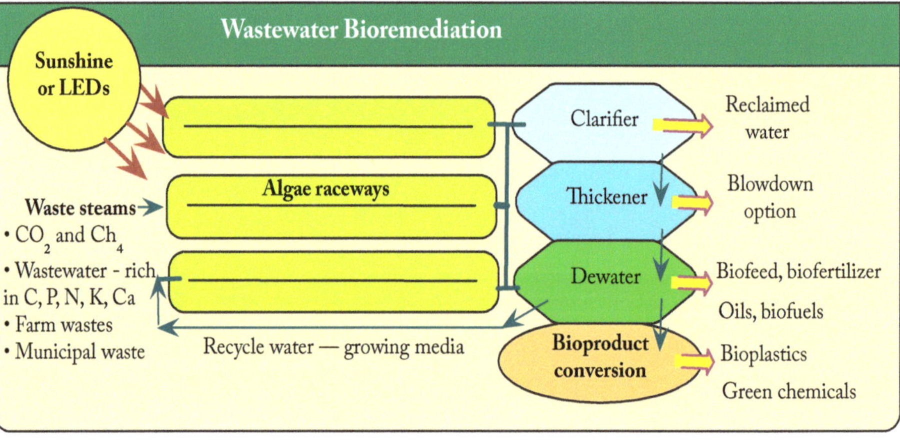

The secondary effluent remains loaded with inorganic nitrogen and phosphorus, which causes eutrophication and a host of other problems. Algae can clean this water by using the power of photosynthesis to absorb waste nutrients, primarily nitrogen and phosphorus and transform them into clean biomass. Algae provide a tertiary biotreatment as the cells remove heavy metals, as well as some toxic organic compounds from the water. Algae culture offers an elegant solution to water pollution, avoids secondary pollution, and results in clean water. In many areas of the world, clean water has more value than the algae biomass.

What are Environmental Benefits for the Green Friendship Bridge?

Puerto Rico

Puerto Rico provides a case study for environmental, health benefits as well as disaster relief. Puerto Rico has a population of about 3.5 million US citizens in an area a little larger than of Delaware. Hurricane Maria, a powerful Category 5, 50-mile wide hurricane with 150 mph winds hit Puerto Rico on September 20, 2017. Three months later, over 86% of the 3.4 million US citizens were without power, the largest power outage in American history. Recovery efforts were slow. Over 300,000 residents moved to Florida by the end of 2017.

The storm destroyed over 90% of agricultural production and the infrastructure for future food production – roads, leveled land and irrigation. Without infrastructure, farmers cannot produce field crops. Unfortunately, when ecological disasters occur, countries seldom have the means to buy replacement food for their hungry population. With roads and bridges destroyed, distributing available food becomes problematic. However, microfarms can be diffused quickly because they do not require traditional agricultural infrastructure.

Disaster relief

Possibly the strongest economic value microfarms offer, beyond sustainable jobs and a healthier local population, is fast response to disasters. Earthquakes, tsunamis and volcanoes can create ecological and economic catastrophes. Climate chaos amplifies droughts and temperature spikes that kill field crops, wildfires and fierce storms demolish crops.

A common element of disaster is an abundance of wastewater, but lack of clean water and food. Peace microfarms packaged in a box can be delivered to disasters sites quickly and provide clean water and fresh healthy food locally in a matter of weeks. Container-based microfarms are not available yet, but are under development.

Disasters create waste water and botanicals

Unlike food deliveries that must be repeated weekly, microfarms can sustain local families and communities indefinitely. The Power On Puerto Rico project provides an excellent disaster recovery model for charging small electronics off the grid. The Amicus Solar Cooperative, a solar energy cooperative, and Amurtel, an international disaster relief nonprofit, is sending 100 off-grid Solar Outreach Systems to Puerto Rico.

Peace microfarm growers can produce food and clean water quickly following a disaster. Growers can use abundance methods with wastewater and sunshine to produce food, biofertilizer, biofeed and even medicines. Growers can do not need inputs from the central government to continue reliable food production for years.

Microfarms have a natural life of about 10 years. Smart monitors, the growers' network and preventive maintenance can assure sustained productivity. After 10 years, it is a relatively simple and cheap process to replace the polycarbonate container and liner, as well as any worn pumps and piping.

What are Environmental Benefits for the Green Friendship Bridge?

Even before hurricane Maria, nearly 50% of rural children and the elderly in Puerto Rico suffered from malnutrition. After the hurricane, 4-year-old boy who weighed just 6.3 kilograms, (13.8 pounds) died in December at San Juan's Pavia Hospital. Peace microfarms distributed across the country can resolve malnutrition and many of the associated diseases.

The Algae Dome designed by SPACE10 provides a microfarm example that may combat chronic malnutrition. SPACE10's project, displayed in 2017 in Copenhagen CHART art fair, may combat malnutrition, greenhouse gases and moderate deforestation. IKEA's future living lab worked with bioengineer, Keenan Pinto and three architects, Aleksander Wadas, Rafal Wroblewski and Anna Stempniewicz to build a photobioreactor that facilitates high production of algae that can be grown almost anywhere on the planet.

Summary

Distributed local food production offers many advantages for health and ecology. The Federation des Spiruliniers de France illustrates how various producers can thrive, even in climate zones not optimal for algae production.

The 2017 hurricane season shows how disasters can leave millions very hungry, thirsty and destitute. Peace microfarms can mitigate disasters by allowing microfarmers to produce healthy food and clean water locally.

8. What are Ecological Benefits for the Green Friendship Bridge?

NAFTA and U.S. farm subsidies artificially reduced crop prices lower than Mexican farmers could produce, forcing thousands of families into bankruptcy. Many other farmers were forced off their land when their irrigation water that they had depended on for generations ran out when flows from U.S. rivers dropped to a trickle. Even the tiny flows were often unusable due to agricultural fertilizer and pesticide pollution and salt percolated from U.S. irrigation. Mexican farmers were forced to abandon the farms many had held for generations, because the scarce water was too salty or polluted to grow crops.

Why did Mexican farmers immigrate north?

The Colorado River is one of the principal rivers of the Southwestern U.S. and northern Mexico. The 1,450-mile Colorado River drains an expansive, arid watershed that encompasses parts of seven U.S. and two Mexican states before reaching the Gulf of California. Unfortunately, the extended Rocky Mountain drought and expanded demand from seven U.S. states' cities and farmers consume nearly all the river water before it gets to Mexico.

The "doctrine of prior appropriation" governs water law in most western states. The first person to make "beneficial use" of water gains the right to use that quantity for that purpose forever. The first beneficial use claim takes precedence over every claim made later. Large tracks of U.S. farmland have claims that pre-date cities. Those farmlands take their full allotment every year, leaving no water for Mexican farms.

The Colorado River provided irrigation water for Northern Mexican farmers for decades. In recent years, the stream into Mexico has slowed to a trickle. Water has flowed to its natural outlet at the upper end of the Gulf of California only once since the 1990's. Each time irrigation water evaporates, additional salt is left to invade downstream farms. People who drive into or out of the town of San Luis Río Colorado, in the state of Sonora, complain about having to pay a six-peso toll to cross a bridge that spans sand.

San Luis Río Colorado Bridge, Sonora Mexico

The minimal Colorado River water flowing into Mexico, when it flows, is extremely salty. Salt and other minerals left from irrigation evaporation migrate to the river and amplify salinity. Runoff from farms and treated waste from cities are channeled back into the river adding more salt, industrial chemicals and discarded pharmaceuticals. Heavy use of agricultural chemicals and pesticides along the Colorado River further pollute downstream water and degrade soils, springs, creeks and aquifers.

The other major river Mexican farmers has depended on for irrigation has also been tapped by U.S. farmers before it the water gets to Mexico. The Rio Grande, or Rio Bravo del Norte in Spanish, serves as part of the natural border between the U.S. state of Texas and the Mexican states of Chihuahua, Coahuila, Nuevo León, and Tamaulipas. Since the mid–20th century, heavy water consumption of farms and cities along with many large diversion dams on the river has left less than 20% of its natural discharge to flow to the Gulf.

As the rivers dry, many springs and creeks in northern Mexico have gone dry. Aquifers have crashed as the water table recedes. When water for crops becomes either too degraded to use for crops or totally unavailable, farmers are forced to move off their land. Entire rural communities have had to move when household water became unavailable when their wells went dry.

Food without fresh water

Peace microfarms can produce excellent edible protein using some forms of waste, brackish or brine water. Algae recycle and reuse the nutrients in the water and transform them to green biomass. Algae grown in waste or other water containing heavy metals cannot be eaten but may provide valuable biofertilizer.

These production systems are insufficient to provide food by themselves but can supplement other scarce food supplies. Of critical importance, microfarms can provide the essential nutrition necessary to assure the avoidance of malnutrition for pregnant mothers and infants. Several microfarm applications designed for environmental benefits require production of algae species other than spirulina.

Technology will be available soon to use peace microfarms to clean some types of waste or brine water. Half the water stored on the planet is brine water and many algae species thrive in saline or brackish water. Numerous brine water aquifers are distributed throughout Mexico and Central America. Algae has been used in the U.S. for wastewater treatment for over 50 years. In some communities, algae's ability to clean water may be more valuable than the production of food, feed, biofertilizer or nutraceuticals.

Algae biofertilizer

Decades of crop production, cultivation, irrigation and erosion from wind and water have degraded and worn out substantial regions of cropland. Many farmers do not have sufficient money to buy agricultural fertilizer and degraded soils require increasing amounts of fertilizer to produce acceptable yields.

Few farmers have access to the 10 tons of organic material needed for composting one ton of fertilizer recommended by the USDA. Even if massive amounts of organic wastes were available, most farmers have neither the heavy equipment nor the diesel available to cultivate organic material into the soil. Organics spread on top of the ground do not deliver enough fertilizer to crops because most the nitrogen volatizes into the air. Organic material such as animal or human manure typically has too many pharmaceuticals to use as crop fertilizer because

those pharmaceutical molecules are likely to be absorbed into the the food crop.

Algae are tiny cells, often about 5-microns in diameter. These small cells cannot absorb a huge pharmaceutical molecule. Instead, the tiny cells strip the molecule of individual elements, especially carbon, which detoxifies the pharmaceutical. Therefore, when the algae biofertilizer enters a food crop, there is no pharmaceutical molecule left to enter the crop, only the bionutrients needed by the plant.

Algae can recover and recycle the nutrients in wastewater very efficiently and deliver the nutrients in a form immediately bioavailable to field crops. Field studies have shown farmers can cut chemical fertilizer costs 50 to 80% with algae biofertilizer.

A two-year field study with Del Monte Fresh Produce demonstrated the value proposition for algae biofertilizers. We extracted two algae species from an abandoned 200-acre field near Yuma bounded on three sides by Arizona raw desert. The field was worn out from years of crop production, cultivation, compaction and salt invasion.

The desert soil was extremely compacted with a pH of 9.4. We cultivated an indigenous terrestrial cyanobacteria, blue-green algae to fix nitrogen from the air, along with green algae to deliver nutrients to the cantaloupe crop. We selected algae in situ because those algae have adapted over eons for survival in the extreme heat, sometimes 125° F. The algae were grown together in a mixatrophic system near the field. A simple ¼ inch hose fed the algae culture to a small canal that fed the field's drip system.

Terrestrial algae

The microfarm provided substantial value by minimizing fossil inputs, increasing productivity and reducing costs. The Del Monte field study exceeded the metrics reported in the table below. The comparisons are to a nearby control field and Del Monte's field norms. Microfarmers can use algae biofertilizers to improve soils and reduce water, energy and fertilizer waste.

Fossil inputs. Eliminate or minimize scarce and expensive fossil inputs including fresh water, fossil fuels, fertilizers, and fossil agricultural chemicals.

Plentiful inputs. Produce valuable biofertilizers and plant growth hormones using solar, wind or other green energy, CO_2, and wastewater.

Reduce water. Enhance soil humus by 50%, water holding capacity, for a 25% reduction in needed irrigation. Algae continue to grow in the soil, as long as moisture is available, which substantially enhances soil organics and fertility.

Reduce fertilizer. Save over 50% on fertilizer costs.

Improve plant stress tolerance. Crops germinate and survive 30% more effectively despite prolonged heat, extreme storms, salt invasion and pests.

Germination algae biofertilizer versus control

Reduce chemicals and pesticides. Algae biofertilizers enable plants to produce their own natural growth hormones and biopesticides.

Eliminate or minimize chemical pesticides and poisons. Algae growth hormones stimulate plants to produce natural pesticides and other protective mechanisms to discourage predators.

Boost yield and quality for field crop farmers

Texture and taste. Improve produce texture and taste through the immediate bioavailability of micronutrients. A blind taste test at ASU resulted in a 17:1 preference for the algae biofertilized fruit versus a nearby control field.

Productivity. Improve crop yield, speed to maturity, size, weight and quality 30-50% by providing the full spectrum of immediately bioavailable nutrients.

Vitamins and minerals. Enhance the presence, quality and availability of vitamins and minerals 20-30% in produce with bioavailable nutrient and micronutrient delivery.

Reduce costs. Transform a cost, waste, to a profit center that reduces crop input costs.

Regenerate soils

Soil compaction. Reduce soil compaction and increase porosity 500% to stimulate root growth, make room for microflora and worms to enhance plant strength.

Crust. Strengthen soil crust with nutrients and organic material that minimize erosion.

Soil structure. Improve topsoil structure by expanding the humus and organic material in the soil. This enhances water retention and nutrient absorption.

Soil microbes. Use algae to attract microbial communities that act symbiotically to enhance crop health, productivity and nutralence.

Soil fertility. Improved porosity allows salts to percolate below the root zone, thus reducing the crop burn from soil salt invasion.

Improve agroecology

Pollution. Reduce air, soil and water pollution by using fewer chemical fertilizers.

Erosion. Minimize topsoil loss to wind and water.

Ag chemicals. Minimize pollution and residues on produce from agricultural poisons.

Nutrients. Deliver bioavailable nutrients to roots precisely when plants need them.

Greenhouse gases. Reduce GHG emissions, especially CO_2, methane and nitrogen oxides.

Tillage. Reduce the need for tillage 50% to reduce soil disruption, compaction and erosion.

Organic farming. Support and accelerate the transformation from industrial farming to sustainable organic farming.

Algae Microfarm Benefits for Farmers

Possibly the strongest attribute of algae biofertilizers may be the ability to repair degraded and even abandoned soils. More research is needed to quantify the microfarm size required to support specific acreage. A 50 m^2 (544 ft^2) surface area microfarm should produce enough biofertilizer to support about 200 hectares, (500 acres) of crop production. This repair function provides a critical need in nearly every food growing region globally.

Larger melons with algae biofertilizer

Farming is hard on soils as each crop extracts about half the applied fertilizer while the other half percolates below the root zone or erodes on the wind. Algae biofertilizer replaces nutrients and rebuilds humus, thus upgrading degraded soil with every crop. Increasing soil porosity enables substantially better root structure and depth, which improves water and nutrient uptake. Porosity also allows an influx of helpful symbiotic microflora communities.

Environmental summary

Pease microfarms distributed throughout Central America and Mexico can make a huge environmental difference for farmers and for the local ecology. Farmers and their families could make a living while providing healthy, nutritious food for their community.

Each microfarm can grow enough biofertilizer to support about 200-hectares of field crops. Algae biofertilizers can improve crop yields 20 to 40% while improving size, color, taste and texture. Microfarms can cut fertilizer costs by >50%, water >25%, fuel >25%, (due to less need for cultivation), and pesticides by 80%. Biofertilizers have demonstrated 40% higher germination rates, 30% better survival rates and 10% faster growth to maturity.

Instead of continually subtracting and degrading soil, farmers can improve soil structure and fertility with every crop.

9. Do USA families deserve a Green Friendship Bridge?

Prior chapters highlight the value proposition for building a Green Friendship Bridge of peace microfarms in lieu of 1%, (13 miles) of Donald Trump's proposed border wall with Mexico. If a friendship bridge of peace microfarms were built for Mexican and Central American farmers, should another bridge be built for U.S. families in impoverished rural communities and urban food deserts?

are surprising and includes: New Orleans, Chicago, Atlanta, Memphis, Minneapolis, San Francisco, Detroit, New York and Camden, New Jersey, (the Garden State). New Orleans has only 20 supermarkets now compared with 30 before hurricane Katrina.

Though food deserts are prevalent in the Mid-Atlantic and the South, the USDA projects that large swathes of the Midwest and West Coast

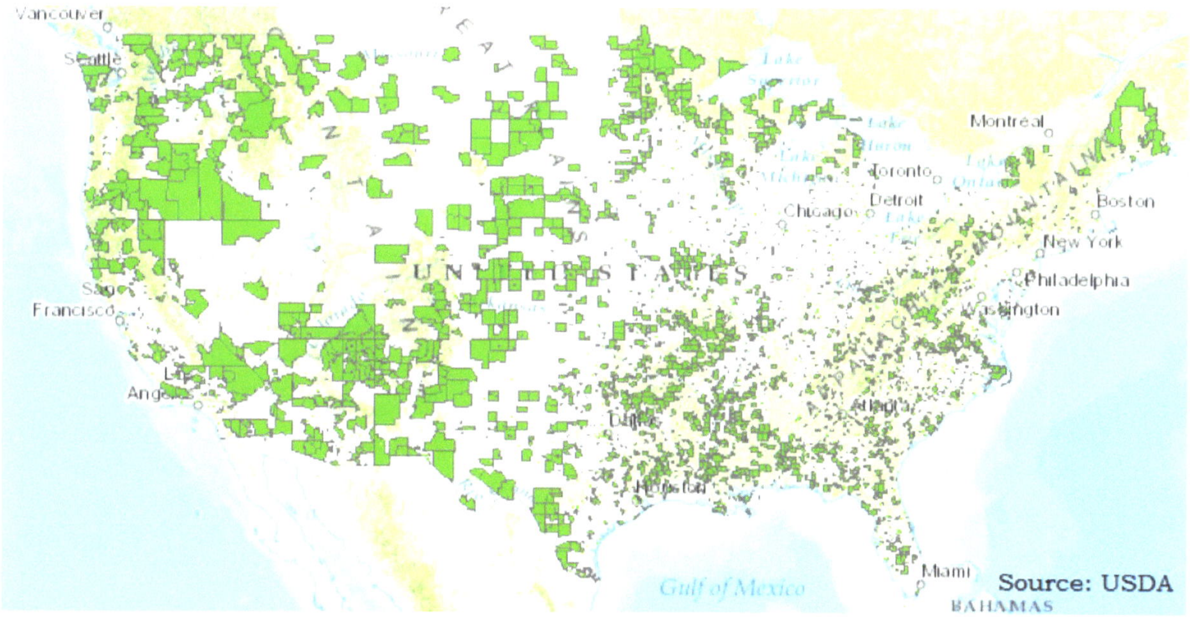

Rural household rates of food security in the U.S. are generally higher than urban households. The irony is that many of these food-insecure households are in the rural and farm communities whose productivity feeds the world and provides low-cost wholesome food for American consumers. Rural families are hit doubly hard because they are also exposed to the substantial dust, pesticide and agricultural poisons that flow from industrial agricultural crop production. In many rural areas, agricultural pollution also degrades surface and well water.

Over 25 million Americans, including 6.5 million children live in food deserts, where they are more than 10 miles from a supermarket. These families do not have easy access to good nutritional choices, including fresh vegetables and fruit. The cities with the worst food deserts

also struggle to meet Americans' food accessibility needs. The USDA recently published a map of food deserts in the U.S.

Food insecurity in the U.S.

About 1 in 5 children in the U.S., 15.5 million, are food-insecure. One in three children receives food assistance via the food stamp program called the Supplemental Nutrition Assistance Program. Over 48 million Americans live in food-insecure households in a country gifted with perfect weather and lands for excellent food crops. Over 5.4 million seniors over age 60, or 9% of all seniors are food insecure.

Food insecurity exists in every county in the U.S., ranging from a low of 4% in Slope County, ND to a high of 33% in Humphreys County, MS. The top ten states leading in food insecurity are states that produce considerable food, including Mississippi, Arkansas, Louisiana, Kentucky, Texas, Ohio, Alabama, Missouri, North Carolina and Oklahoma. These states are blessed with considerable sunshine and warm temperatures that are ideal for peace microfarms.

Hidden hunger and malnutrition

Many American's suffer from hidden hunger due to an over-abundance of calories but have severe nutritional deficiencies. Often obese children and adults are malnourished because they consume the wrong types of foods. Empty calorie foods such as many snacks, soft drinks, candies, and desserts foods deliver lots of calories but practically no critical nutrients. Hidden hunger robs millions of Americans of the opportunity to reach their full potential.

Micronutrient deficiencies occur when people eat enough calories, but fail to get essential nutrients such as vitamins and minerals. Malnutrition is common in developing countries but also has become common in the U.S. Hidden hunger deprives children of the essential nutrition they need to reach their full physical and cognitive potential.

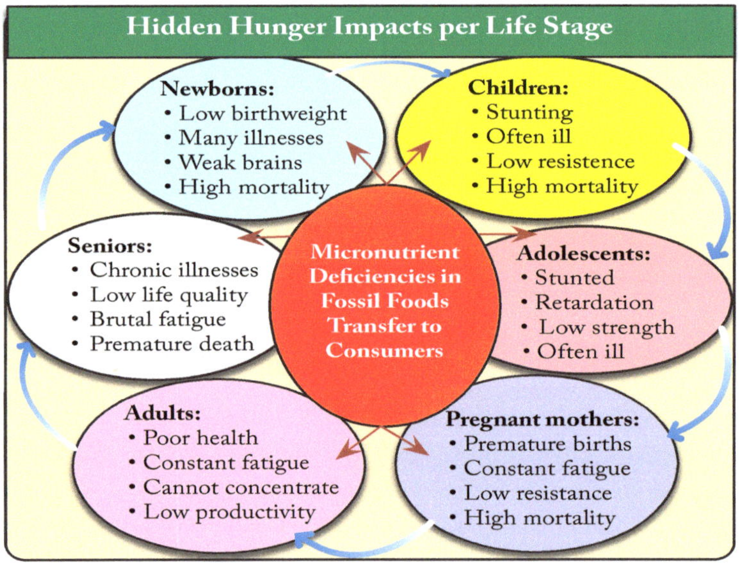

Hidden Hunger impacts – Source: UNICEF

More than 50% American children do not get enough of vitamins D and E, while more than a quarter do not get enough calcium, magnesium or vitamin A, according to a recent Journal of Nutrition study.

Malnutrition leaves children extremely vulnerable to illness and infection. It can also lead to higher levels of aggression, hyperactivity

and anxiety, or the reverse, fatigue and lethargy. Malnutrition diminishes brain function and degrades a developing child's ability to learn. These micronutrient deficiencies result in a compromised immune system, stunted physical growth, reduced mental ability, lifelong chronic disease and premature death. Infants who lack micronutrients can develop stunted critical organs, which compromises their lives.

Undernutrition imposes horrific human and economic tolls. Children lack the energy to pay attention in school, drop out prematurely and become dependent on social services for life. Vitamin and essential nutrient deficiencies add billions to U.S. healthcare costs. These health care expenses combined with the loss in productivity and wages for those who are sick, as well as higher assistant living costs, impose an estimated annual $157 billion drag on the U.S. economy.

A microfarm can provide the critical nutrients for an entire community. Local microfarms can eliminate malnutrition, hidden hunger and food insecurity in the U.S.

Pregnant mothers

Mothers to be need about 300 calories more than their normal diet and they need more protein, Vitamins A, C, D and B9, iodine and calcium. Studies have shown that women who get 400 micrograms (0.4 milligrams) of folate daily *before* conception and during early pregnancy reduce the risk that their baby will be born with a serious neural tube defect. These birth defects involve incomplete development of the brain and spinal cord by up to 70%. Folic acid, sometimes called folate, is a B vitamin (B9) found mostly in leafy green vegetables like kale and spinach, orange juice, and enriched grains.

The most common neural tube defects are:

- Spina bifida, an incomplete closure of the spinal cord and spinal column.

- Anencephaly, severe underdevelopment of the brain.

- Encephalocele, when brain tissue protrudes out to the skin from an abnormal opening in the skull.

These birth defects happen during the first 28 days of pregnancy — usually *before* a woman even knows she's pregnant. Therefore, women of child bearing age need sufficient folic acid in their diets or as supplements. Mothers also need about 250 micrograms of iodine a day to help ensure the development of the baby's brain and nervous system.

Antenna Technologies spirulina production

Spirulina for moms

Spirulina offers a strong nutritional source for potential mothers. The micro-vegetable contains about 60% protein and is a complete protein containing all essential amino acids. A 100 gram, (3.5 oz, about a tablespoon) of spirulina supplies 290 calories and is an excellent source (20% or more of the Daily Value, DV) of numerous nutrients, particularly B vitamins (folate, thiamin and riboflavin, 24%, 207% and 306% DV, respectively) and vitamin E (24% DV). It also supplies dietary minerals such as iron (219% DV) manganese (90% DV), potassium (29% DV) and zinc (21% DV). Spirulina's 8% lipid content by weight provides excellent antioxidants beta carotene, gamma-linolenic acid, alpha-linolenic acid, linoleic acid, stearidonic acid, eicosapentaenoic acid, docosahexaenoic acid, and arachidonic acid.

Malnutrition solutions

Only 100 g of spirulina given to malnourished infants over 8 weeks cures them of malnutrition. This model uses about 2 g of spirulina a day per child and requires only about 100 g of dried spirulina total for each child.

Spirulina provides substantial health benefits for people of all ages. The phycocyanin, polysaccharides, antioxidants and phytonutrients in a 3-gram spirulina serving per day:

- 60% protein and an excellent source of vitamins A, K1, K2, B12 and iron, manganese and chromium.

- Health-giving phytonutrients such as carotenoids, GLA, SOD and phycocyanin.

- 2800% more beta-carotene than carrots, 3900% more iron than spinach.

- 600% more protein than tofu and 80% more antioxidants than blueberries.

This nutritional profile leads to a wide array of health benefits, including:

- Strengthened immune system and boosted energy level.

- Supported cellular, cardiovascular, eye and brain health.

These health and vitality benefits assure microfarmers of strong markets for their valuable micro-vegetables, (algae biomass).

Metrics

Field experience in Africa demonstrates that a 50 m², (544 ft²) microfarm yields about 135 kg of spirulina per year. Antenna's research shows that an 8-week spirulina treatment with 100 g (total) resolves childhood malnutrition. Therefore, each microfarm can deliver enough spirulina to cure **1,350 children** and/or pregnant mothers from the horrible impacts of malnutrition. Many locations in the US can double the productivity of rural Africa. Therefore, each microfarm can serve a substantially larger community.

The 14,000 peace microfarms in the U.S. Green Friendship Bridge could cure **19 million US children and pregnant mothers** from malnutrition each year.

Homeland Security

Food security and avoidance of malnutrition is a worthy goal because it helps not only the kids, our next generation, but their families, schools, medical facilities and communities. Stronger kids grow up to be better citizens and to be strong contributors to local economic prosperity.

The US Armed Forces should view healthy children strategically. Food insecure and malnourished children have neither the mental nor the physical capability to serve. A Mission Readiness report estimates that 75% of young American adults cannot meet the armed forces' academic and physical health standards for recruits.

Algae strategies to prevent overeating

Studies show that sodium alginate reduces plasma glucose and protects the antioxidant system in diabetics. Alginic acid and other compounds in sea vegetables exert a protective effect against diabetes. Alginic acid may improve the sensitivity of cells to the action of insulin, thereby improving glucose tolerance and normalizing blood sugar. Sodium alginate induces significantly lower postprandial rises in blood glucose, serum insulin and plasma C-peptides. The addition of sodium alginate in the diet leads to a delayed gastric emptying rate induced by the fiber, which moderate glucose response. Algae polyphenol extracts have anti-diabetic effects through the modulation of glucose-induced oxidative stress. These extracts slow starch-digestive enzymes such as alpha-amylase and alpha-glucosidase.

Obesity and diabetes

Algae compounds provide a wide array of medical benefits for children plagued with obesity and diabetes. Two unique strategies may be called "fill-gut" and "gut-full signals."

The **fill-gut** strategy adds a few grams of dried algae eaten early in a normal meal, possibly as sprinkles on a salad or drink. Algae expand and fill the stomach. Alginates absorb 300 times their weight in water, which quickly fill the gut and suppresses appetite by sending the gut-full signal to the brain.

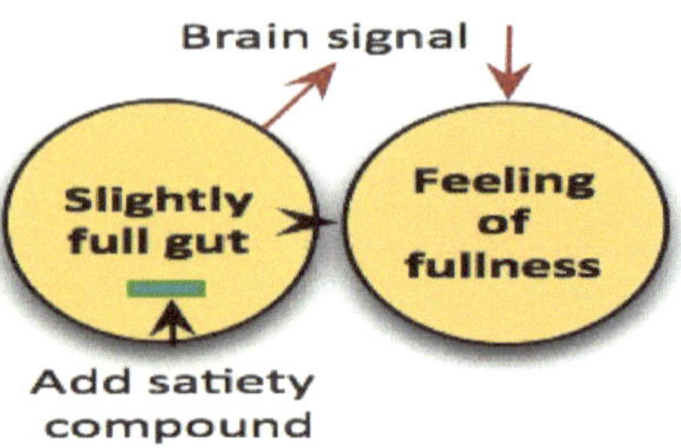

Gut-full signals work because algae compounds activate the stomach's natural **satiety** signals. Satiety signals an immediate feeling of fullness, which tells the eater to stop eating naturally. Algae satiety signals the brain and quashes the nosh feeling.

U.S. peace microfarm summary

Peace microfarms distributed throughout the U.S., particularly targeting poor rural areas and urban food deserts can make a huge difference for families and communities. Peace microfarms can end food insecurity, hidden hunger and malnutrition in many communities.

Peace microfarms offer a superb legacy: preserve our precious natural resources for the next generation. Since growers continually recycle carbon and nutrients, they not only save money but also preserve diminishing natural resources.

Algae foods can moderate the obesity and diabetes epidemic in the US, which the CDC estimates cost >$150 billion annually. Algae can provide nutritious foods that make consumers feel satiety rather than the nosh feeling that leads to more eating.

The U.S. Green Friendship Bridge will provide Americans with incredible health and nutrition benefits. In addition, peace microfarms will yield tremendous payback from social, economic, environmental and sustainability advantages that accrue to millions of people who live in food deserts or are too poor to be able to afford nutritious food for themselves and their family.

10. Path Forward: Green Friendship Bridge

Currently, political discussions focus on how much Trump's Wall will cost and who pays for it. DHS has responsibility for Trump's Wall and will pay for the wall with borrowed money. Waste of funds on a wall means other, more valuable actions such as education, healthcare and alleviation of poverty and malnutrition in America, will have less funding.

A much wiser discussion might focus on whether Trump's Wall makes sense. Why build a wall?

1. A benefit analysis shows substantially negative value.

2. The number of illegal border crossings has dropped by the end of 2017 to the lowest point in in 17 years.

3. Net immigration today flows south, not north.

4. ICE captures fewer immigrants each month because fewer are trying to cross the border.

5. Kumar Kibble, deputy director of ICE, testified before the House Subcommittee that "ICE spends $12,500 to arrest, detain, and remove an individual from the United States."

6. Homeland Security experts have testified multiple times that enough wall has been installed.

7. DHS officials have testified that in remote regions, the wall does no good.

8. Multiple congressional members, both Democrats and Republicans, have testified that enough wall has been installed.

9. Experience has shown that the current barriers provide only a nuisance for border crossers.

10. Each new study predicts Trump's Wall will cost more and add several billion a year in maintenance costs.

11. Due to insufficient U.S. capacity, the U.S. would have to buy the cement from Mexico, the rebar from China and create a miracle to find enough water to make the cement to build the wall.

12. Human-caused climate change produces more fierce storms that produce floods, which will destroy large parts of the wall.

13. There is no practical way to site a wall along the 1,254 undulating miles of the Rio Grande River.

14. Over 36 federal laws had to be waived to build the existing wall. In addition to environmental laws, the current fence violates the Farmland Protection Policy Act, the Religious Freedom Restoration Act, and the Native American Graves Protection and Repatriation Act.

15. The Tohono O'odham Nation's reservation spans 75 miles of the US-Mexico border. A tribal vice-chairman declared "The whole idea behind it is just racist." He said, "The government would build the wall over my dead body."

16. An July 2017 survey by the Associated Press-NORC Center for Public Affairs Research found that 58% of Americans oppose new spending for the border wall.

17. America has at minimum, 1,000 infrastructure projects that should take priority over Trump's Wall.

Trump's Wall represents and incredibly simply a stupid waste of money. If it were not for Trump's repeated campaign promises, the wall would not be in conversation.

Friendship Bridge

The Green Friendship Bridge proposes to shift 1% of the cost for Trump's proposed wall to build 14,000 peace microfarms. The Friendship Bridge will advance freedom and peace rather than constructing an ugly and largely useless barrier.

Peace microfarms, provided with training to farmers and families scattered across Mexico and Central America, will create jobs, reduce malnutrition and improve health. Peace microfarms will enable families to produce good food locally so they do not have to migrate north.

U.S. farm policies, especially commodity subsidies, forced much of the migration from Mexico and Central America. The Friendship Bridge may motivate the U.S. to change the harmful agricultural policies. The U.S. Friendship Bridge can save natural resources, reduce pollution and restore many degraded ecosystems.

Centralized agricultural production and long distribution channels create severe problems in the U.S. too. A second Friendship Bridge to Rural America will benefit the 20% of U.S. children that are currently food insecure. The U.S. Green Friendship Bridge can resolve food security, malnutrition, obesity and diabetes for millions of Americans.

Peace microfarms will lead to spontaneous creativity led by ordinary citizens expressing themselves with extraordinary imagination. Microfarms will become more productive as farmers innovate and develop better methods. Superb nutrition will make children, families and communities healthier and improve their vitality. Microfarms will not only enable farmers and families to produce highly nutritional food locally, but also improve local ecosystems.

Peace microfarms offer substantial social, economic, health and environmental benefits for families and communities in the U.S. as well as for our neighbors south of the border. We need to begin diffusing peace microfarms now!

Mark R. Edwards, Dr. Metrics

Mark cultivates microcrop miracles to pursue food justice and resolve poverty and hunger.

He facilitates Ana's path to assure health and vitality for those in need, locally and globally. *The Green Friendship Bridge* is his 15th book in the *Green Algae Strategy Series*, focused on affordable, sustainable and safe food and energy.

Mark graduated from the U.S. Naval Academy, where he earned degrees in engineering, oceanography and meteorology. Jacques Cousteau motivated and mentored his interest in the oceans and global stewardship. He holds an MBA and PhD in strategic marketing and consumer behavior and taught sustainability, food marketing, engineering, leadership and entrepreneurship at ASU for 39 years. He cofounded the Sustainable Phosphorus Initiative at ASU, which has grown into the #1 global source for phosphorus R&D and policy.

He served as marketing director for the Pritikin Longevity Institute, where he helped design healthy foods and lifestyles. As a director for a Fortune 50 food company, he did a series of projects designed to create functional foods with krill and farmed shrimp and salmon. He has performed extensive R&D on new foods and consumer adoption of novel foods.

Mark founded and served as CEO of the software and assessment firm TEAMS Intl. for 22 years. He invented dozens of advanced metrics, including 360° feedback, that are used today by firms globally. He has consulted for Disney, 3M, Monsanto, DuPont, Nabisco, Quaker Oats, General Mills, Borden, Coca-Cola, Frito-Lay, GE, Intel, J&J, Merck, GM, Bank of America, and most of the food / agribusiness companies. He speaks international on advanced metrics, innovation and sustainable food and energy.

Mark has published over 140 articles and 26 books that span business and science disciplines. His *360° Feedback*, with partner Ann Ewen, was a business best seller. Several science books won international best science and environment awards including *Green Algae Strategy*, *Abundance: Sustainable fossil-free Food*, *The Tiny Plant that saved our Planet*, *Freedom Foods* and *Peace Microfarms*.

Universities in over 30 countries use several of the *Green Algae Strategy* series books in food, energy and sustainability courses. He writes the popular *Algae Secrets* blog for *Algae Industry Magazine*.

The Green Algae Strategy Series focuses on creating Sustainable and Affordable Food and Energy – "SAFE" production. Teachers, professors and policy leaders use Green Algae Strategy books in schools and colleges in over 30 countries for courses in sustainability, engineering, business, politics, social entrepreneurship, food, water, energy, ecology, environment and world future.

BioWar I: Why Battles Over Food and Fuel Lead to World Hunger, 2007. BioWar I, where food is burned for fuel, must be ended by withdrawal – not of soldiers, but of damaging agricultural subsidies.

Green Algae Strategy: Engineer Sustainable Food and Fuel. 2008. Algae offer solutions for sustainable and affordable food and energy because algae are the most productive biomass source on Earth. ***Best Science Book* – 2009, Independent Publisher Awards.**

Green Solar Gardens: Algae's Promise to End Hunger, 2009. Algaculture in small but beautiful solar gardens and algae microfarms distributed globally will enable SAFE production locally.

Crash: The Demise of Fossil Foods and the Rise of Abundance. 2010. Fossil-based agriculture sits precariously on a foundation of unsustainable fossil resources that will become unaffordable and then will run out. Abundant agriculture is sustainable because it uses plentiful inputs that are cheap and will not run out.

Smartcultures: Nature's tiny Genius – Algae – Reverses Pollution and Regenerates Degraded Ecosystems, 2011. Farmers may recycle farm wastes to their fields using abundance microfarms. Smartcultures give 20 – 30% higher yields by providing bioavailable nutrients at just the right time. Farmers save 30 – 40% by reducing input costs and reduce ecological pollution by 90%.

Abundance: Sustainable Fossil-free Foods with superior Nutrition and Taste; less Pollution and Waste, 2010. Abundance presents the value proposition for algae food, feeds and other forms of energy using plentiful resources that will not run out. Abundance growers can clean the air and water while they grow foods with superior nutrient density and better sensory values,

including color, texture and taste. **Pinnacle Gold Medal winner 2011, Best Environmental Book.**

The tiny Plant that saved our Planet. The incredible true story of Al. Al saved our planet by eating the bad carbon genie, which enabled the earth to cool and gave us oxygen. If we educate our children, maybe they will prompt us to take action — now. **Nautilus Silver Medal winner 2011, Best Children's Book.**

Abundant Agriculture: Smartcultures enable superior Nutrition and Yields from Regenerated Fields, 2010. Abundant agriculture represents the first new form of agriculture in 60 years. Abundant agriculture produces sustainable food, feed, fiber and other coproducts using primarily non-fossil resources,

Freedom Foods: Superior Nutrition and Taste from low on the Food Chain for People, Producers and Our Planet, 2011. Freedom foods liberate consumers to make healthier food choices. Freedom foods are sustainable and grow free of fossil resources, GMO material and agricultural chemicals and pesticides.

Imagine Our Algae Future: **Visionary Algae Architecture and Landscapes**, 2012, with Robert Henrikson. See visionary images from the AlgaeCompetition.com showing how algae will change our world. Contestants from 40 countries created amazing graphics, pictures and videos showing how algae is produced today and will be used tomorrow for food, feed, biofuels, medicines and ecological repair.

Peace Microfarms: A Green Algae Strategy to Prevent War. 2015. Wars are fought over food and the fossil resources required to produce food. Peace microfarms enable growers to use abundance growing methods that use no or minimal fossil resources to produce freedom foods. Peace microfarms can avoid war and save our precious resources for future generations.

Ana Feeds Our World by 2040: Miracles with Nature's Nano Cell Biofactory. 2017. The next food renaissance will engage green biotechnologies that produce healthier foods with minimal or no fossil resources. Freedom Foods liberate growers from fossil resource consumption and deliver superior nutrition and taste without pollution and waste.